INTRODUCING ROMAN DECLAMATION

INTRODUCING ROMAN DECLAMATION

A NEW CULTURAL AND ANTHROPOLOGICAL PERSPECTIVE

MARIO LENTANO

TRANSLATED AND EDITED BY
WILLIAM MICHAEL SHORT

UNIVERSITY
of
EXETER
PRESS

First published in 2023 by
University of Exeter Press
Reed Hall, Streatham Drive
Exeter EX4 4QR
UK
www.exeterpress.co.uk

Copyright © 2023 Mario Lentano

The right of Mario Lentano to be identified as author of this work has been asserted by him in accordance with the Copyright, Designs and Patents Act 1988.

Translated and edited by William Michael Short

https://doi.org/10.47788/OMCZ3540

British Library Cataloguing in Publication Data
A catalogue record for this book is available from the British Library

ISBN 978-1-80413-101-5 Hardback
ISBN 978-1-80413-102-2 ePub
ISBN 978-1-80413-103-9 PDF

Cover image: Funerary relief found in Neumagen near Trier, a teacher with three discipuli, around AD 180–185, Rheinisches Landesmuseum Trier, Germany. https://commons.wikimedia.org/wiki/File:Funerary_relief_found_in_Neumagen_near_Trier,_a_teacher_with_three_discipuli,_around_180-185_AD,_Rheinisches_Landesmuseum_Trier,_Germany_%2829656302165%29.jpg

Typeset in Adobe Garamond Pro by S4Carlisle Publishing Services, Chennai, India

CONTENTS

	Introduction	1
1	Declamation: a short history	5
2	The practice of declamation and rhetorical education	17
3	Themes and characters	24
4	Culture in declamation	40
5	The politics of declamation	59
6	Declamation and law	72
7	Greeks and Romans	81
	Bibliography	91
	Index	105

INTRODUCTION

> I set forth notions that are human and my own,
> simply as human notions considered in themselves,
> not as determined and decreed by heavenly ordinance
> and permitting neither doubt nor dispute.
> *Michel de Montaigne*

This book is intended for university students as well as scholars who may be unfamiliar with Latin declamation. By way of a brief overview, it gives the reader a reasonably precise idea of this fascinating but underappreciated aspect of ancient education. Despite renewed interest in scholastic rhetoric since the 1990s, which has finally freed the discipline of its (already ancient) ostracism from scholarship, *controversiae* and *suasoriae* remain the domain of a highly circumscribed specialist circle. Although almost three hundred complete texts have been preserved for us, they have been almost entirely marginalized in textbooks, and academic studies—though increasing yearly—are still very far from covering every aspect of the field.

The silver lining is that in research on Roman school rhetoric there is still vast area for exploration around controversial questions on which the academic community has not yet reached consensus. What is more, these questions regard not only minor aspects or *cruces* of a textual-critical nature (no matter how relevant these may be), but also key themes, such as the relationship between declamation and its political context(s); between academic jurisprudence and practical legislation; between formative training and effective forensic practice (towards which training was directed). There is even much debate around what meaning should be attributed to declamation, understood as a didactic practice and also as a foundational educational and cultural experience that continued throughout the imperial period to influence the aristocracy. What the ramifications of this experience might have been for the diffusion of specialized knowledge, for the creation of a common imaginary, and for the elaboration of an élite world-view, are still not easily judged.

Consequently, in this book I will often take a position on some of these questions—not only highlighting current scholarly debates on unsettled problems, but also stating explicitly which among the marshalled arguments I view as more persuasive and compelling. Bibliographic references allow the interested reader to evaluate this position in the context of other coherent or conflicting interpretations. In this respect, I want to state immediately that the bibliography at the end of the book is not meant to be exhaustive on the subject of Latin declamation. Rather, it aims to highlight some of the most important recent scholarship where it is possible to find references to earlier literature, as well as discover the names of scholars working internationally in areas of scholastic rhetoric. More comprehensive references can be found in the now abundantly available bibliographic resources that cover both declamation in general and the specific authors to whom the various texts available to us have been attributed (often only traditionally).[1]

Furthermore, I want to clarify that this brief introduction has been intentionally and selectively organized according to three distinct profiles. In the first place, I am interested in the declamations as *texts*: the concretely compiled "themes" that make up the major and minor anthologies of Seneca the Elder, Pseudo-Quintilian, and Calpurnius Flaccus. Dozens of declamatory *argumenta* are present in Quintilian's seminal *Institutio oratoria* and more can be found in the massive late antique rhetorical manuals. But this body of work is usually limited to citations, notes, and possible themes for *controversiae* or *suasoriae*, often illustrating one or another type of legal case. Normally, they do not offer any extended development of arguments, providing only scattered or terse indications whose elaboration is left to the schoolmasters for whom these manuals were intended.

Second, our interest rests almost exclusively on aspects of the content of declamation. It is well known that scholastic rhetoric had its own particular style, with its series of formal solutions that exerted significant influence on literature throughout the imperial period. But such considerations rest outside this book's scope; the reader may consult the many studies already available, beginning with the unsurpassed (though hardly empathetic) writing of Eduard Norden and continuing through the more recent work of Bé Breij and Emanuele Berti.[2]

A final (but particularly serious) limitation has to do with the choice to examine only Latin works. As a school practice, declamation originated in Greece and in the imperial period became a phenomenon across the entire area dominated by Rome, equally in the eastern territories and in the western Latin-speaking areas. Authors such as Libanius and, in the Byzantine period, Choricius of Gaza—to name only two—offer written themes in large number and of great interest, lending themselves to comparison with what was being produced contemporaneously in the West. Experts, arguments, and norms of

---

1 Cf. esp. Lentano (1999 and 2017a).
2 Cf. Norden (1986), vol. I, 281ff.; Breij (2006a); Berti (2007).

Introduction

the spurious declamatory jurisprudence circulated in equal measure from one end of the empire to the other, generating hybrids and reciprocal influences and justifying recourse to the idea of a *koiné* for referring to the phenomenon. In the period of Seneca the Elder—who preserves some material dating back, in the oldest layers, to the period of the second triumvirate—Greek and Roman rhetoricians work side by side in the same schools, participate in the same debates, and discuss the same themes. Despite this, a comparative study of Greek and Roman declamation remains, for the moment, forthcoming. The last chapter of this book, titled "Greeks and Romans", broaches this question to some degree, discussing some examples and sketching out some lines of possible research, but does not exhaust it. In the rest of the book, I have preferred instead to privilege scholastic rhetoric as it developed within a specific cultural context, that of the Roman world.

Despite these limitations, I am confident my efforts have been worthwhile and that they may encourage other researchers to scrutinize a body of Roman society's intellectual output that still has much to reveal about itself and the culture that produced and cultivated it for so long—a body of work whose importance can be inferred from, if nothing else, the fact that it contributed for centuries to the formation of the class that actively administered the empire, produced or commented on its laws, wrote its literature, and in turn educated its successors.

Mario Lentano

I wish to thank my dear friends and teachers Graziana Brescia and Maurizio Bettini for once more taking on the thankless task of reading the manuscript of this work and for having improved it by suggestions, critiques, and comments. Neither can be held responsible in any way for the inevitable mistakes a work such as this will contain; they have the merit, instead, of having reduced their number and limited their frequency. I requested the help of Emanuele Berti and Giunio Rizzelli for specific sections of the book and received precious commentary from them. I am also grateful for the help of Nicola Basile, Alfredo Casamento, Giuseppe La Bua, Jon E. Lendon, Lucia Pasetti, Alessandra Rolle, and Antonio Stramaglia in providing a bibliography. A final thanks to my colleague and friend William Michael Short for his invaluable translation.

I note that the critical editions used for the texts of the declamations are those of Lennart Håkanson for Seneca the Elder and for Calpurnius Flaccus (respectively 1989, and 1978), for the *Declamationes minores* that of Michael Winterbottom (1984), which I prefer to the more recent but more interventionist Shackleton Bailey (2006), and for the *Declamationes maiores* that of Antonio Stramaglia (2021), with the translation by Michael Winterbottom. Other translations, unless otherwise indicated, are my own.

I

DECLAMATION: A SHORT HISTORY

Cicero declaimed not what we today would call "controversies", nor indeed what before his time were defined as "theses": the genre in which we practice our exercises is in fact so novel that even its name is new! We speak of "controversies"; Cicero called them "cases". To tell the truth, their other name is Greek—"scholastic"—but translated into Latin it ended up taking the place of the native term; the word "controversy" is instead much more recent, just as "declamation" cannot be found in any author before Cicero and Calvus. Calvus distinguished declamation from diction: he claims, in fact, to be only an elegant declaimer, but a good speaker, and believes that the first term refers properly to private exercises, the second to real trials. The name is relatively new and the associated practice has only recently come into vogue: for this reason, it is not difficult for me to know, from its very beginnings, a phenomenon that was born after me.[1]

This passage, which opens the anthology of declamations circulated by Seneca the Elder at the beginning of the reign of Caligula, represents the first and the most articulated ancient reconstruction of the origins of declamation. Its author was a famous equestrian who came from the Roman colony of Cordoba in Spain, where he was born around the middle of the first century BCE. In his youth, he had been a student of the schools of rhetoric, a close friend of Porcius Latro—a fellow Spaniard—and of other famous teachers of the late Republican and Augustan period. Seneca frequented the world of rhetoricians for most of his very long life. He tirelessly listened to, took notes from, and sketched profiles

---

[1] *Controversiae*, 1, pr. 12: Declamabat autem Cicero non quales nunc controversias dicimus, ne tales quidem quales ante Ciceronem dicebantur, quas thesis vocabant. Hoc enim genus materiae, quo nos exercemur, adeo novum est, ut nomen quoque eius novum sit. Controversias nos dicimus: Cicero causas vocabat. Hoc vero alterum nomen Graecum quidem, sed in Latinum ita translatum, ut pro Latino sit, "scholastica", controversia multo recentius est, sicut ipsa "declamatio" apud nullum antiquum auctorem ante Ciceronem et Calvum inveniri potest, qui declamationem <a dictione> distinguit; ait enim declamare iam se non mediocriter, dicere bene; alterum putat domesticae exercitationis esse, alterum verae actionis. Modo nomen hoc prodiit, nam et studium ipsum nuper celebrari coepit. Ideo facile est mihi ab incunabulis nosse rem post me natam.

of the most prominent teachers and students. In old age, he decided to put into writing the mass of material he had accumulated throughout his life in a work that he dedicated to his three children (among them the philosopher who would later become Nero's teacher). The declared aim of this work was, among other things, to preserve an inheritance of oratorical talent that, owing to the circumstantial nature of its creation, risked being lost once the generation of first-hand witnesses had passed.

Seneca produced a book unique in the whole panorama of ancient literature. It is not just an anthology of over seventy years of scholastic rhetoric, overseen by an intellectual who knew that world intimately and deeply. In passages "by the author", Seneca mixes in anecdotes about this or that person, scenes from the daily life of rhetoric schools, accounts of debates and attacks that proliferated in that narrow and often self-referential world, and critical profiles of the best (and also the worst) orators known to or followed by him.

Seneca thus appears to occupy an ideal observation post for reconstructing the history of a cultural phenomenon, scholastic rhetoric, that he was able to observe both from afar and up close. In reality, his work is marred by a series of imprecisions and omissions. Among the most significant is his claim that Cicero was unfamiliar with that brand of exercise later known as declamation. Seneca himself (in 1.4.7) reports a theme of controversy undertaken by the statesman from Arpinum that is entirely of a piece with the others in his anthology.[2] Furthermore, Seneca is completely silent on the Greek precedents of declamation, which in the final analysis go back to Athenian sophists of the fifth century BCE, at least indirectly, and to the marked rhetorical interests of the Peripatetic School.[3] And yet, even with such undeniable mistakes in his reconstruction, Seneca was not wrong to consider declamation "born after him".

In the Roman world, teachers of rhetoric—mostly Greeks—were active from the first half of the second century BCE. As proof, there is an act of the Senate of 161 BCE empowering the praetor to banish rhetoricians and philosophers from Rome.[4] This appeared in the context of the lively cultural battle of those decades, when the mass infiltration of Greek culture into Rome as a result of the recent eastern conquests provoked the reaction of an aristocracy that was anxious about contact with an intellectually unscrupulous and corrosive tradition of thought, infinitely more advanced than Rome's—and because of this was rejected by those who saw in it a possible threat to Rome's traditional morals and to the power structures supported by those morals.

---

2 As has been recently shown by Berti (2009).
3 Excellent information in Fairweather (1991), 104–31 and more briefly in Berti (2007), 110–114.
4 The text of the decree is preserved in Suetonius, *De grammaticis et rhetoribus*, 25.2.

The same hostile attitude can be observed in the edict of 92 BCE in which the censors Gnaeus Domitius Ahenobarbus and Lucius Licinius Crassus expressed their disapproval of the school of the so-called Latin rhetoricians, active in Rome at the time and where, for the first time, the teaching of rhetoric was imparted in Latin. In the text of the act (known to us through Suetonius), the censors fulminated against this "entirely new kind" of school, in which young Roman men—this is what occurs to the two authoritative magistrates—passed their time in leisure. They conclude that "Our ancestors established once and for all what they wanted their sons to learn" and that "we do not like this novelty, which goes against tradition".

It is not hard to imagine what lies behind these repressive efforts. At the beginning of the first century BCE, rhetorical training involved long and costly stays in the capitals of the Hellenistic East, where famous teachers imparted their lessons, in Greek, to the offspring of an élite scattered to the four corners of the Mediterranean. This curriculum, already strongly selective in itself, was associated at home with the so-called apprenticeship of the Forum (*tirocinium fori*), the custom by which young men attached themselves to established orators to learn their trade, meant to provide future members of the governing aristocracy with a moral as well as professional education. In both cases, access to forensic activity and the acquisition of knowledge necessary for launching a political career had a markedly censorial character. In particular, this apprenticeship allowed the ruling class to choose its successors, exercising a critical role in the co-optation of new members of the élite. In this context, we can understand why the efforts of the Latin rhetoricians, to the extent that they could "democratize" access to a strategic base of knowledge and thus deprive the aristocracy of its filtering role, was abhorred by a part, at least, of the ruling class, whose preoccupations the censorial act of 92 BCE explicitly embodies.

Things changed dramatically in the second half of the first century BCE. Perhaps thanks to measures such as Caesar's to grant Roman citizenship to anyone moving to the city as a teacher, and to new efforts by the Augustan principate to enlarge the administrative and governing class, the schools of rhetoric began a period of intense growth.[5] And though Greek teachers continued to be important at that time, these were now accompanied by teachers of the Latin language, and pedagogy was in Latin. Certainly, some of the Greek rhetoricians active in Rome must have spoken Latin perfectly and must have enjoyed Roman citizenship: if we did not have biographical information from Seneca the Elder, we would never know that men of letters such as Caestius Pius and Arellius Fuscus, who

---

5 Suetonius, *Divus Iulius*, 42 reports the episode.

declaimed in Latin and had fully Roman names, actually came from the Greek-speaking area of the empire. From this moment on, the rhetorical schools became a sort of obligatory rite of passage for anyone with the means to undertake those studies; and declamation would end up exerting a profound influence on literature, on the culture in general, and on the imaginary of the imperial age.

Students landed in the rhetorical schools—roughly equivalent to our secondary schools—after an apprenticeship in a plethora of "preliminary exercises" (*progymnásmata* in Greek; *praeexercitamina* in Latin), understood as preparation for the most important and most complex practices, those of *suasoria* and of *controversia*.[6] Progymnastic manuals have reached us almost exclusively from the Greek world.[7] As regards the Latin schools, we have only seven complete *suasoriae* preserved by Seneca the Elder, and about three hundred *controversiae* across four *corpora* gathered by Seneca the Elder (about eighty pieces), by Pseudo-Quintilian (*Declamationes minores*, about a hundred and fifty pieces, and *Declamationes maiores*, nineteen pieces) and by Calpurnius Flaccus (*Declamationum excerpta*), whose original collection we possess only in an epitome made in a later period, containing fifty-three extracts.

The only corpus whose author and chronological positioning we can identify with certainty is the *Oratorum et rhetorum sententiae, divisiones, colores* of Lucius Annaeus Seneca the Elder, or Seneca Rhetor (we have already sketched his biographical profile). Since Seneca knew of the death of the Mamercus Aemilius Scaurus, in 34 CE, by Tiberius's command, and because he cites fragments of the historian Cremutius Cordus, whose work, banned by Tiberius, was recirculated by Caligula in 37 CE, we can assume that he published his work under this emperor, when he was about 90 years old. Here it may be worth adding that Seneca was also the author of an historical work, the *History from the Beginning of the Civil Wars*, which was inspired by the idea that the history of Rome followed a parabolic, almost biological, trajectory in which it was possible to identify an infancy, a phase of growth, the reaching of maturity (coinciding with a culmination of strength and power), and the later arrival of a process of decline, reaching its culmination in the collapse of the Republic. Given Seneca's convictions about the value of school rhetoric (an interesting but futile genre) and of historiography (an intellectually "high" genre, involving the search for truth), it is reasonable to aver that it was in his historical work that he trusted his hopes of living on in fame—a hope destined to remain unfulfilled, given that the *Historia*, published posthumously by Seneca the philosopher under

---

6   Cf. the complete list of these exercises in Berardi (2017).
7   There is now a very useful English translation, with an excellent introduction, in Kennedy (2003).

Caligula, succumbed to the same fate that deprived us of a great part of Latin historiography of the imperial age and is now known only fragmentarily. By contrast, his rhetorical work has survived almost completely, even if a portion of the original ten books (plus one of *suasoriae*) has only reached us as extracts.

Our information is much worse about the two anthologies transmitted by the manuscript tradition under the name of Quintilian (Marcus Fabius Quintilianus). Quintilian was a Spanish lawyer and rhetorician, who under Vespasian and his sons Titus and Domitian held the chair of eloquence established by the emperor and maintained by the treasury, and was author of a manual in twelve books, *The Orator's Education* (*Institutio oratoria*), which contains precious theoretical reflections on scholastic rhetoric and a large collection of sample themes. Many scholars also attribute to Quintilian the *Minor Declamations*, comprising originally 388 pieces but reaching us in sharply reduced number from the first part (beginning from 244). Whatever the case, they probably belong to the school he was in charge of, likely a sort of textbook by a teacher who was trained there, as suggested by its numerous points of contact or even full correspondence with the teachings and overall didactic orientation expressed by Quintilian himself. Recently, on this question, Antonio Stramaglia has suggested that the *Minor Declamations* are a teaching text, similar to the *Division of Questions* of the Greek rhetorician Sopatros and datable to the end of the first century or, more likely, the beginning of the second century CE.[8] Both texts give us a glimpse of an ancient teacher as he explains to his students how to construct a declamation.

The question of the nineteen *Major Declamations* is more complex. These are complete, polished, ready-to-run pieces. Compared with the *Major Declamations*, the texts of the *Minores* seem like partial rough drafts. The collection was published at the end of the fourth century CE, perhaps in 384, but the pieces it includes, wrongly attributed to Quintilian, were composed from the early second to the first half of the third century CE by different authors and are distinguishable from one another by stylistic and formal criteria.[9] We also possess titles of and fragmentary information about other declamations circulating under the name of Quintilian but rejected from the curated collection at the end of the fourth century.[10] As always when speaking about ancient literature, what has survived is only a very small portion of what was originally a larger set, the outlines of which we struggle to grasp.

---

8 Cf. Stramaglia (2010).
9 Extensive information in Schneider (2000); Stramaglia (2006); Håkanson (2014), 47–130, and now Santorelli (2021).
10 Complete details in Santorelli and Stramaglia (2015), 287–294, and now Stramaglia (2017).

Introducing Roman Declamation

We can say very little about the *Declamatory Extracts* (*Declamationum excerpta*) of Calpurnius Flaccus, in part because there is a difficulty in keeping distinct the epoch of composition of the original collection and that in which the epitome that has reached us was made. It seems reasonable to date it within the second to third centuries CE, as suggested by recent lexical analysis.[11]

The three collections of Pseudo-Quintilian and of Calpurnius Flaccus contain only *controversiae* and thus fictious legal cases. By contrast, the Senecan anthology preserves some examples of *suasoriae*, exercises in which an imaginary figure from myth or history is addressed in order to persuade them to complete (or avoid) some choice. Following, I give as examples the themes of three of the seven *suasoriae* preserved by Seneca:

> The three hundred Spartans sent against Xerxes deliberate whether to flee, after the other groups of three hundred sent by the Greek cities decide to do so.[12]

> Alexander the Great debates whether to enter Babylon, after the augur's response prophesying a danger he should be on guard against.[13]

> Cicero deliberates whether to throw his own writings into the fire, following a promise of immunity from Antony if he should do so.[14]

By comparison with the *controversiae*, whose connection with judicial oratory and with the sphere of law was very strong, the *suasoria* had a markedly "deliberative" character. The abilities it imparted were among those required, especially in the Republic period, by senators in their role of guiding the decisions of the highest Roman institution or by magistrates in controlling turbulent popular assemblies. Of course, under the principate those abilities were not superfluous. Under Augustus, and thereafter increasingly throughout the imperial period, the real locus of decision-making was in the imperial court, and in particular among the entourage of advisors closest to the *princeps*. The *amici Caesaris* or *consilium principis* took on a well-defined role in making the great choices that marked the reign of this or that emperor. Not by chance, in the *suasoriae* it was almost always a political leader of the highest rank who had to be pushed in one direction or another.

---

11 Balbo (2016), 63. Santorelli (2017), 139 proposes the second half of the second century.
12 *Suasoriae*, 2: Trecenti Lacones contra Xerxen missi, cum treceni ox omni Graecia missi fugissent, deliberant, an et ipsi fugiant.
13 *Suasoriae*, 4: Deliberat Alexander Magnus, an Babylona intret, cum denuntiatum esset illi responso auguris periculum.
14 *Suasoriae*, 7: Deliberat Cicero, an scripta sua comburat promittente Antonio incolumitatem, si fecisset.

Declamation: A short history

The second exercise of scholastic rhetoric is very different. In *controversiae*, at the pinnacle of rhetorical education, the student was presented with a fictional (and often quite complex, even quite improbable) legal case, and was asked to speak on behalf of one or another party to it, with the only rule that he must adhere to the questions in the theme of the controversy itself. Teachers would propose themes for debate (in Latin *thema*, a Greek term, but also *argumentum* or *propositio*), and describe the imaginary event on which the controversy turned. Soon, many of these themes congealed into more or less fixed formulae that went unchanged for centuries, proposed time and again to each new generation of students. Usually, themes were limited to a rough sketch of events and relations, leaving to the rhetoricians the job of fleshing out the individual figures and of speculating about the reasons motivating their behaviour. The result is what Seneca calls *color*, that is, the particular "inflection" given to the treatment, the guideline that shaped the accusation, and the defensive strategy developed by students. Besides the details of the theme, the student proposed a plan of work (*divisio*), grounded in the first instance in classification of the case within a general typology, according to a framework developed in the great rhetorical manuals (the so-called *status*, discussed in Chapter 2). Finally, along with the theme, the opening of a *controversia* included the laws that should guide discussion (Chapter 6) and establish the rights and prerogatives of the contestants or fix the legal frame of their contest (indicated in italics in the declamation themes that follow).

I now provide only a very small specimen of the around three hundred *controversiae* that have reached us, namely the themes of the eight declamations that comprise Seneca the Elder's first book:

1. *Sons should support their parents or be put in chains.* Two brothers are in conflict. One has a son. The young man's uncle falls on hard times and he begins to support him, despite his father's prohibition. Disinherited because of this, the son makes no complaint. He is then adopted by his uncle, who thereafter becomes rich by inheritance. In turn, the young man's father falls on hard times, and he supports him, despite his uncle's prohibition; he is disinherited by his uncle.[15]

2. *A priestess should be chaste and of chaste parents, pure and of pure parents.* A virgin is abducted by pirates, then sold to a pimp who compels her into

---

15 LIBERI PARENTES ALANT AUT VINCIANTUR. Duo fratres inter se dissidebant. Alteri filius erat. Patruus in egestatem incidit. Patre vetante adulescens illum aluit. Ob hoc abdicatus tacuit. Adoptatus a patruo est. Patruus accepta hereditate locuples factus est, egere coepit pater; vetante patruo alit illum. Abdicatur.

prostitution. With her clients, she successfully obtains payment through entreaty: when a soldier tries to take her by force, she kills him in the scuffle. She is taken to court, absolved, and restored to her parents. She stands as a candidate to the priesthood.[16]

3. *A priestess who violates her oath of virginity should be thrown from the Tarpeian Rock.* A priestess, condemned for violating her oath of virginity, invokes the help of Vesta before being thrown from the Tarpeian Rock. She survives the fall. Repetition of the punishment is requested.[17]

4. *Whoever finds an adulterer in flagrante delicto with the adulteress, will not be guilty after killing both. It is allowed for a son to punish the adultery of his mother.* A war hero has lost both hands in battle. He finds his wife, with whom he has a son (now a young man) with her lover; he orders his son to kill them both. The son does not kill them and the adulterer escapes. The war hero disinherits his son.[18]

5. *A violated woman should choose between the death of the perpetrator or marriage to him without a dowry.* In a single night, a man rapes two women: one asks for his death, the other for marriage.[19]

6. Taken prisoner by pirates, a man writes to the father to be ransomed, but the father does not ransom him. The daughter of the pirate captain makes him swear that he should take her as his wife, if he was freed; he swore it. Leaving her father, the girl follows the young man; he returns to his father and marries her. A woman with an inheritance appears. The father orders the son to divorce the daughter of the pirate captain and to marry the woman. The father disinherits him when he refuses.[20]

---

16 SACERDOS CASTA E CASTIS, PURA E PURIS SIT. Quaedam virgo a piratis capta venit; empta a lenone et prostituta est. Venientes ad se exorabat stipem. Militem, qui ad se venerat, cum exorare non posset, colluctantem et vim inferentem occidit. Accusata et absoluta remissa ad suos est; petit sacerdotium.
17 INCESTA SAXO DEICIATUR. Incesti damnata, antequam deiceretur de saxo, invocavit Vestam. Deiecta vixit. Repetitur ad poenam.
18 ADULTERUM CUM ADULTERA QUI DEPRENDERIT, DUM UTRUMQUE CORPUS INTERFICIAT, SINE FRAUDE SIT. LICEAT ADULTERIUM IN MATRE ET FILIO VINDICARE. Vir fortis in bello manus perdidit. Deprendit adulterum cum uxore, ex qua filium adulescentem habebat, imperavit filio, ut occideret: non occidit, adulter effugit. Abdicat filium.
19 RAPTA RAPTORIS AUT MORTEM AUT INDOTATAS NUPTIAS OPTET. Una nocte quidam duas rapuit. Altera mortem optat, altera nuptias.
20 Captus a piratis scripsit patri de redemptione; non redimebatur. Archipiratae filia iurare eum coegit, ut duceret se uxorem, si dimissus esset; iuravit. Relicto patre secuta est adulescentem. Redit ad patrem, duxit illam. Orba incidit: pater imperat, ut archipiratae filiam dimittat et orbam ducat. Nolentem abdicat.

7. Sons should support their parents or be put in chains. A man kills one of his brothers because he was a tyrant, another because he had found him in adultery with his wife, even though the father begged him to save him. Captured by pirates, he writes to the father to be ransomed. The father then sends a letter promising he will give the pirates double what was asked for if they cut his hands. The pirates free him. When the father falls on hard times, the son refuses to maintain him.[21]

8. Whoever has fought in combat heroically three times should be released from further military service. A father tries to restrain his son who has fought heroically in battle three times and wants to return to battle again; he disinherits him when he refuses.[22]

This is only a small sample. We will have occasion to cite other themes later to enrich this sketch. However, certain patterns emerge that are repeated throughout the world of school rhetoric: consistent laws, even if they are occasionally inflected according to very different situations (such as the one that requires children to support their parents, or the one, unwritten but presumed in many of the cited themes, that empowers a father to disinherit a child for various reasons); stock characters, such as the pirate or the war hero (*vir fortis*); conflict between family members owing to adultery; and so on. Similarly, we see the outlines of important questions posed by each of these texts. Only in very few cases do such questions have to do with law in the strict sense; more often, the juridical framing represents a sort of pretext for confronting problems of an anthropological kind: whether there are behaviours of a father so serious as to obviate a child's duties to him, or if the child is nevertheless required to support the father; what is meant by "purity" and "chastity"; to what degree a father can interfere in his children's marital choices; whether you must obey a father who orders you to kill your mother, even if she is adulterous or begs to be spared; and so on.

As we have seen, for Seneca the *controversia* was a recent phenomenon, the invention of which he considered himself to be an eyewitness. Other sources, including Suetonius's *Grammarians and Rhetoricians*, make a distinction between "new" and "old" declamations, and provide succinct exemplification of these typologies. So far as we can tell from Suetonius, controversies originally had to

21 LIBERI PARENTES ALANT AUT VINCIANTUR. Quidam alterum fratrem tyrannum occidit, alterum in adulterio deprehensum deprecante patre interfecit. A piratis captus scripsit patri de redemptione. Pater piratis epistulam scripsit : si praecidissent manus, duplam se daturum. Piratae illum dimiserunt. Patrem egentem non alit.
22 QUI TER FORTITER FECERIT, MILITIA VACET. Ter fortem pater in aciem quarto volentem exire retinet; nolentem abdicat.

do with cases taken from history or from concrete forensic situations, often with precise factual or geographic indications. Sometime later, the themes began to take on the form known to us from the four aforementioned collections, and this can already be seen in the eight themes cited earlier. Their events no longer take place in Rome or indeed in any specific place, but in an undetermined city conventionally called Sophistopolis, the "City of Rhetoricians", to borrow the definition proposed for Greek declamation by Donald Russell.[23] Its inhabitants were generic fathers, sons, war heroes, pirates, tyrants and tyrannicides, stepmothers, all rigorously anonymized—arranged by the declaimers like so many pieces on a chessboard, in all possible configurations and according to a limited set of "moves". The result is fathers and sons being imprisoned within an endless oscillation between obedience and conflict; pirates invariably abducting unsuspecting sea travellers and holding them for ransom; stepmothers represented as ferocious enemies or incestuous lovers of their stepsons; tyrants despotically exercising their power until struck down by tyrannicides; tyrannicides, like any *vir fortis*, in conflict with the city from which they seek recognition and compensation for a heroic deed that goes against the laws of Sophistopolis, and so on. Not to mention all those themes in which the situation is tinged with fantasy—magic potions, the living dead, tombs rejecting the bones of patricides, oracles demanding human victims to end a pestilence—or that touch on the belligerent and macabre—with poisoned drinks, bodies dissected in the search for a cure, or desperate citizens feeding on the cadavers of those who perished before receiving their coveted dole of wheat. These features become increasingly distinct the further we penetrate into the mature period of the principate, in homage to the taste for fantasy and "pulp" that is identifiable in other literary genres as well, such as epic, tragedy, the novel, and even biography. If this be true, Seneca's claim that declamation—in the form in which he had known it and appreciated it for his entire life—was younger than himself was well founded.

At the same time, the picture we have sketched also accounts for the criticism that has been lodged against school rhetoric since antiquity and which was most effectively synthesized in the opening pages of Petronius's *Satyricon*:

> Are our rhetoricians tormented by another tribe of Furies when they cry: "These scars I earned in the struggle for popular rights; I sacrificed this eye for you: where is a guiding hand to lead me to my children? My knees are hamstrung, and cannot support my body"? Though indeed even these speeches might be endured if they smoothed the path of aspirants to oratory. But as it is, the sole result of this bombastic matter and these loud empty

---

23 Russell (1983), 21–39.

phrases is that a pupil who steps into a court thinks that he has been carried into another world. I believe that college makes complete fools of our young men, because they see and hear nothing of ordinary life there. Yes, it is pirates standing with chains on the beach; yes, tyrants writing edicts ordering sons to cut off their fathers' heads, yes, and oracles in time of pestilence demanding the blood of three virgins or more, honey-balls of phrases, every word and act besprinkled with poppy-seed and sesame.[24]

Even Quintilian, who understands that declamation as a practice has already become deeply rooted in the curriculum, who believes it is undeniably useful for educating future orators, fights to bowdlerize it and to expunge its most improbable features. He observes: "In laws and in praetorian edicts, we would search in vain for soothsayers, pestilences, oracles, stepmothers crueller than those of tragedy and many other things even more incredible".[25] From here it is a short step to questioning the function of controversies in a school system designed, above all, to prepare the future orator for the realities of the Forum. And Petronius's sardonic statement that declaimers felt bewildered and as if in another world when they finally reached the Forum suggests this step was taken very early.

But an anthology of ancient and modern judgements of declamation would be too easy and of very little actual interest. In the following pages, we will instead have two objects. First, we will try to understand how the narrative world of the rhetoricians works; who its inhabitants are; the conflicts they are embroiled in; and the sets of rules that are established for negotiating these conflicts and for allowing parties to those conflicts to express their rationales. Second, we will formulate hypotheses about the value and complex meaning of declamatory education and the effects it likely had on those who undertook it in the crucial years of their intellectual formation. Declamation must have been

---

24 Petronius, 1 (trans. of E.H. Warmington): Num alio genere Furiarum declamatores inquietantur, qui clamant: "Haec vulnera pro libertate publica excepi; hunc oculum pro vobis impendi: date mihi ducem, qui me ducat ad liberos meos, nam succisi poplites membra non sustinent"? Haec ipsa tolerabilia essent, si ad eloquentiam ituris viam facerent. Nunc et rerum tumore et sententiarum vanissimo strepitu hoc tantum proficiunt ut, cum in forum venerint, putent se in alium orbem terrarum delatos. Et ideo ego adulescentulos existimo in scholis stultissimos fieri, quia nihil ex his, quae in usu habemus, aut audiunt aut vident, sed piratas cum catenis in litore stantes, sed tyrannos edicta scribentes quibus imperent filiis ut patrum suorum capita praecidant, sed responsa in pestilentiam data, ut virgines tres aut plures immolentur, sed mellitos verborum globulos, et omnia dicta factaque quasi papavere et sesamo sparsa. A recent analysis appears in van Mal-Maeder (2012), 2–4.

25 2.10.5: Nam magos et pestilentiam et responsa et saeviores tragicis novercas aliaque magis adhuc fabulosa frustra inter sponsiones et interdicta quaeremus. On Quintilian's attitude toward declamation, see Calboli (2010b).

indelibly impressed in the memories of its students, if the satiric poet Persius could still recall imagining, in his school days, the words of Cato of Utica on the eve of his suicide, and if Juvenal could remember composing a *suasoria* to exhort Sulla to renounce the dictatorship.[26] But beyond this, declamation must have contributed powerfully to the creation of a widespread mental framework—and to the shaping of the whole imaginary of the aristocratic audience that would one day take up key posts in the liberal professions and in the administration of the empire. This is why studying declamation is tantamount to peering into the mind of the class that governed the fortunes of the Roman empire for five centuries.

---

26 Persius 3.44–47 and Juvenal 1.15–17, on which cf. respectively Pirovano (2013) and Santorelli (2016b).

2

THE PRACTICE OF DECLAMATION AND RHETORICAL EDUCATION

Declamation is an educational practice. As such, it is both an exercise aimed at acquiring a set of skills and the operational aspect of a discipline that rhetoricians proposed to instil through *exempla*, embodied by individual controversies. The discipline in question is known as the theory or doctrine of *status*, corresponding to Greek *stásis* and in Latin to expressions such as *constitutio*, used by the anonymous author of the *Rhetorica ad Herennium*. In Greek, this theory was elaborated first within the Peripatetic school, later to be defined in the authoritative but lost *Rhetorical Arts* of Hermagoras of Temnos (second century BCE), whose organization we know from the later manualistic tradition (especially from Cicero, the *Rhetorica ad Herennium*, and Quintilian). Concerning declamation's "genetic" relation to *status* theory, scholarly opinions differ. For a highly authoritative specialist such as Gualtiero Calboli, "declamations developed before the systemization of *status* theory" and were an elaboration of this theory.[1] For Emanuele Berti, declamatory themes were instead created "for illustrating it [*status* theory] in its many ramifications and for providing students of rhetoric case types for exercising its applications". In fact, Berti believes that "it is precisely in this requirement that we can see one of the chief factors determining the development of declamation as a didactic tool".[2]

But what does "*status*" mean in "*status* theory"? Even the definition of this key term has undergone a series of progressive tweaks and is hardy univocal in the sources—just as the identification of the different *status* and their separation into general classes was debated. What we can say is that the typology of the question around which the conflict between the parties of a case revolves is substantially the crux of the issue.[3] From this perspective, the classification attributed by later sources to Hermagoras distinguishes between *status rationales* and *status legales*, the former relating to judgments about the facts at stake in the controversy, the

---

1 Calboli (2007), 39.
2 Berti (2014), 100.
3 Calboli Montefusco (1986) remains fundamental for any deep dive into the material.

latter relating to the legal principles that govern it. "Rational" *status* in turn have an internal division, which we can synthetically reconstruct as follows: there is "conjecture" (*status coniecturalis* or *coniectura*) when there is some question of identifying whether the subject has committed the action imputed to him or not; "definition" (*status finitivus* or *finitio*) comes into play when there is agreement on the identity of the guilty part, but not on the precise definition of the committed act. The broadest and most important "rational" *status*, "quality" (*status qualitatis* or *qualitas*), has to do with cases where there is agreement both on the fact and on its definition, but the guilty party claims to have acted according to the law, or at least justifiably. Because of its broadness, this *status* was in turn variously distinguished as *qualitas negotialis*, not entirely well defined by the theory but relating more to deliberation about the future than to defining past events, or *qualitas iuridicialis*, relating to juridical situations. The juridical quality could be *absoluta* if the accused claimed to have acted completely within the law, without needing to appeal to external justification, or *absumptiva* if innocence were instead to be judged on the basis of "assumed" external elements. Thus, in the assumptive juridical quality, there may be a relevant issue of *comparatio* (it was inevitable to act in one way or another, and the way in which the accused acted was the more just or more advantageous for the group or for a great number of subjects or for the counterparty itself); *relatio* (or *translatio*) *criminis* (the accused acted because provoked by others or by the injured party, which merited the punishment); *remotio criminis* (guilt belongs to something or someone who has compelled the accused to act criminally); or *concessio* (in the absence of other arguments, mitigating circumstances such as chance, compulsion, or necessity could be invoked, or begging the mercy of the court). The last and most vague *status rationalis* is *translatio* or *praescriptio*, consisting of an exception raised by the accused around the legitimacy of the trial—for example, by claiming that the accuser had no right to make the accusation.

The "legal" *status* instead relate to the law and its interpretation. The situations envisaged were again four: *scriptum et voluntas* (or *scriptum et sententia*) when there is a conflict between the spirit and the letter of the law or, as the ancients preferred to say, between the presumed intent of the legislator and the available text, assuming that the former expressed the latter defectively; *leges contrariae*, when there are mutually contradictory laws or contradictory principles within the same law; *ambiguitas*, when the interpretation of a legal text is not immediately obvious; and *ratiocinatio* or *syllogismus*, when there is no apposite law for the situation or an existing legal rule must be applied by analogy.

The system was highly ramified, and some theoreticians classify the *status* of different cases into more minute subdivisions than those defined by the canonical typology. For each of the *status*, there were standard procedures and arguments to rely on. In fact, we must not forget that *status* theory has a part to play in *inventio*, that is, it belongs to that branch of rhetorical training and practice aimed at identifying ("finding") what arguments would be most advantageous to one's case. The declamations served very well for this, since their themes were developed precisely to exemplify this or that *status*.

The link between theory and exemplification is clearly captured in the manualistic tradition of the imperial period, beginning with Quintilian's seminal *Institutio oratoria*. Here is an example from Fortunatianus's *Ars rhetorica*, belonging to the fourth century CE:

> In how many ways does the *status* of "the letter and the spirit" manifest itself? In two: either when one of the parties relies on the written text of the law, and the other on its spirit, or when both parties set aside the written text and debate its intention. When one of the parties appeals to the letter of the law and the other to the spirit, how is it? Here is an example: "*If a foreigner climbs the walls, let him be condemned on a capital charge*. A foreigner climbs the walls and drives back the enemy; he is brought up on charges, but he rejects the charges".[4]

Besides illustrating the convention of broaching a topic through question and response, this extract demonstrates the close relation between the type of *status*—in this case, it is one of the legal *status*, namely that of *scriptum et voluntas*—and a declamatory theme exemplifying it.[5]

The manualistic tradition naturally pursued transparency for didactic purposes. It is worth asking, then, if the nexus between *status* theory and declamatory theme can be observed in the four *corpora* at our disposal. To answer this question, we have only the anthology of Seneca the Elder and the *Declamationes minores* of Pseudo-Quintilian. These are the only collections in which, alongside the text of the controversies, we also find commentary—the most appropriate site for discussing the relation of a certain theme to one of the defined *status*. One example is *Controversia* 7.3 from Seneca's anthology, in which a son, caught pounding up a poison—he claims it is for himself—is brought up on charges of attempted patricide. Here, Seneca informs us that he will not, as normal, explain how the rhetoricians involved in discussing the theme went about deciding on

---

4 1.24 (= 99, 6–13 Calboli Montefusco): Scripti et voluntatis status quot modis fit? Duobus, cum aut prima pars scripto nititur, secunda voluntate: aut cum utraque pars omisso scripto sola voluntate contendit. Cum prima pars scripto nititur, secunda voluntate, quem ad modum? Ut: "Peregrinus si muros ascenderit, capite plectatur: peregrinus muros ascendit, hostes propulsavit, petitur ad poenam; contra dicit".

5 The theme was in fact standard, occurring in identical form in Quintilian 7.6.6–7 as well as in Cicero, *De oratore*, 2.100.

its classification; the controversy was in fact clearly of a conjectural type and belonged to the first of the *status rationales*. Therefore, the only point open to discussion was whether the poison was in fact intended for the father (7.3.6).

In Pseudo-Quintilian's *Declamationes minores*, a section under the rubric *Sermo* ("conversation", "discussion") portrays the "master", as the anonymous rhetorician is conventionally called, speaking in the first person and providing suggestions to students on how to develop a theme in forms that often permit us to see concrete scholastic practice, and indeed almost to catch a glimpse of pedagogy in action.[6] In this controversy, there is a question of goods exchanged between two *socii*:

> I have often repeated to you how you can easily identify the *status* of a case. You know what they are in general. So, first, go through them one at a time, rejecting any that does not clearly apply to the case in question. Then, consider those that remain. And consider in this way: see what question the actor proposes and what the proprietor responds, or the defendant. The question should emerge from this comparison, and it will be the question that indicates the *status*. I am not telling you that you must base yourselves on the first thing that the actor says and on the first response of the counterparty. In fact, the *status* is not inferred from the question first posed, but from the most relevant one.[7]

Of course, the teacher is not always so explicit, and at times his suggestions for the treatment of a theme are furnished more ambiguously. One example can be found in *Declamationes minores* 247, recently highlighted by Antonio Stramaglia:

> *Let a wife inherit her husband's property.* A rich young man commits rape. Before the girl makes her choice, he sends relatives to ask her to marry him. After hearing their pleas, she remains in silence crying. The young man kills himself. Before he dies, she agrees to marry him. Both his relatives and the woman claim his property.[8]

---

6   Cf. Oppliger (2016); Winterbottom (2018); Pasetti et al. (2019), XIV–XXI.
7   320.1–2: Saepe vobis dixi quomodo ad inveniendum statum facillime perveniretis. Qui sint omnes novistis. Primum singulos repetite; sublatis iis quos certum erit non esse, inter residuos quaeremus. Quaerendi autem via haec erit. Videamus quid proponat petitor, quid respondeat possessor vel reus: ex eo quaestio nascitur; ea nobis <statum> demonstrabit. Neque hoc dico, quid primum dicat petitor, quid ille respondeat. Non enim ex prima quaestione ducendus est status, sed ex potentissima. Cf. recently Oppliger (2016), 105.
8   MARITI BONA UXOR ACCIPIAT. Adulescens locuples rapuit. Priusquam optaret puella, misit ad eam propinquos rogatum ut nuptias haberet. Auditis illa precibus tacuit et flevit. Percussit se adulescens. Priusquam expiraret, optavit illa nuptias. Petunt bona propinqui et uxor. Cf. Stramaglia (2010), 147–149.

This case turns on whether the woman can rightly be considered the man's wife, since despite exercising her right to choose between her rapist's death and marriage to him, as recognized by declamatory jurisprudence, the marriage has not been consummated because of the man's suicide. The question is not trivial, as its resolution regards the right of the woman to inherit the dead man's property. In the *Sermo*, the teacher hypothesizes what the *rapta* could say to prove she is the man's wife and how the counterparty might object. He concludes: "All this requires being concentrated in a definition (*finitione*): 'A wife is a woman, attached to a man through marriage, who has gone to live with him.'"[9] Something similar can be said about *Minor* 292, focused on the vague legal category of *causa mortis*, punishable by death. Here, too, the teacher specifies that the question of law posed by the controversy "requires treatment through definition".[10] In both cases, the students understood very well that the *status* to which the rhetorician referred was the *status finitivus*, called also *finitio*, in which a definition of the situation must be proposed (in this case, the status of the protagonist) that is most favourable to the party whose point of view is being expressed.

It is not entirely accurate to say that these kinds of suggestions for constructing arguments are found only in the *Minores*. Recently, Antonio Stramaglia has studied the figure of what he calls the "hidden teacher", examining a series of cases from the *Declamationes maiores* in which students are instructed on discursive strategies, not alongside the text of the declamation (as in the *Sermo* of the *Minores*) but within the oration itself, as if these were "captions" woven into the fabric of the discourse and meant to reveal the "technical" presuppositions that governed its creation.[11] I report one of the many examples given by Stramaglia relating to *status* theory and taken from the sixth *Maior* of Pseudo-Quintilian, in which the conflict involves the fate of a son, who in order to free his father from pirates abandons the mother who has demanded support from him and who, now, after his death, wishes to leave him unburied:

> But what does the law say? A SON WHO ABANDONS HIS PARENTS IN MISFORTUNE IS TO BE CAST OUT UNBURIED. Certainly, all that is in dispute between us in this case, judges, concerns the letter and the meaning of the law: are we to take our stand on its ambiguous phrasing or on our confidence in its intention?[12]

---

9   247.2: Hoc finitione comprehendendum est: "uxor est quae femina viro nuptiis conlocata in societatem vitae venit".
10 292.1: Circa ius illud est, ut finitione tractetur. Cf. Pasetti (2018), 129–134; Pasetti et al. (2019), 478–483.
11 Cf. Stramaglia (2016a).
12 6.11.8: Quae tamen lex est? QUI PARENTES IN CALAMITATE DESERUERIT, INSEPULTUS ABICIATUR. Omnis nobis in hac prorsus causa, iudices, de scripto et intellectu legis contentio est, utrum verborum ambiguitate an voluntatis fide standum sit.

In this case, the veil of declamatory fiction is thin and behind the mask of the speaker—the father who pleads for his son's burial—stands the rhetorician who constructed the discourse and who explains how the case in question should be referred to the legal *status* of *scriptum et voluntas*, suggesting that it is the legislator's intention that must form the basis (and in fact will later form the basis) of an effective defence of the father's position.

References to *status* theory are thus sprinkled throughout the collections of declamations, sometimes in adjoined "didactic" sections that offer hints and suggestions to teachers and students, and sometimes as captions directed to those who attended the recitation of the fictitious discourse. Still, despite the major theoretical relevance of the theory and its very close linkage to declamatory practice, it is telling that the term *status* occurs only once in Pseudo-Quintilian's *Minores* and never in Seneca the Elder's collection, even if Seneca obviously knew the relevant terminology, given that on a couple of occasions he describes a case as *coniecturalis*, thus assigning it to the first of the rational *status* identified by rhetorical theory.[13]

Again, the parallel with Greek tradition as represented by the manual of Sopatros is illuminating. In his *Division of Questions*, Sopatros oscillates between didactic-theoretical sections and short pieces for exemplification, not unlike Pseudo-Quintilian in the *Minores*. However, in Sopatros's work the declamations are not organized casually, but instead follow the order of the *status* that had been established by Hermogenes, the rhetorician whose doctrines from the third century CE onwards had prevailed over Hermagoras's. Thus, Sopatros begins from conjecture and provides at the beginning of each new section the necessary theoretical information, along with a list of the arguments to use in relation to the *status* in question.[14] The controversies of Pseudo-Quintilian, like those of Seneca the Elder, can also easily be referred to the framework of the *status*; in fact, this work has already been done.[15] However, this classification has been accomplished *post factum*, since in those collections, except in very rare cases, there is almost systematic exclusion of material explaining the connection between the declamatory theme and the *status* to which it belongs.

It is difficult to understand why this would be so. Seneca the Elder was not a rhetorician by trade, but rather an amateur—more interested in collecting and transmitting the stylistic adornments of declamatory texts than in their legal and doctrinal technicalities (although he has sometimes been credited with a

---

13 Cf. 7.3.6 and 7.7.10.
14 Winterbottom (1983), 73; Winterbottom (1988), 2–3 and now Kalospyros (2016), 261.
15 For Seneca, cf. Calboli (2003), 73–77; Berti (2007), 115–127; Berti (2014) and (2015); for the *Minores*, Dingel (1988), and now Calboli (2016).

comprehensive understanding of *status* theory).[16] But this is not the case for Pseudo-Quintilian, who was fully versed in the subtleties of the theory and whose *Minores* had an obvious didactic aim. Moreover, at least in one case the "master" explicitly refers to the need to identify the *status* to which a theme belongs and even recommends strategies for correct identification, suggesting that one must not be led astray by the initial rationales of the parties, which often turn on secondary questions. But apart from this, and a few other less formal allusions to *status*, the problem is almost never addressed in the *Minores*. Perhaps this anthology is intended for advanced students, who were capable of recognizing the presence and the action of the theory in the very fabric of the discourse without it having to be made explicit. Perhaps, as Michael Winterbottom has suggested, the opposite is true and the *Minores* were directed at beginners who were too inexperienced and too likely to be confused by the technicalities of theory.[17] Perhaps, as Emanuele Berti has suggested to me, students did not need any prior knowledge of the theory, since learning the *status* went hand in hand with learning to organize a proper *divisio* and to structure an effective *argumentatio*.[18] Or perhaps we should think of the declamations as having their own autonomous value, which is separate from exemplification of this (or any) theory, as well as a discursive complexity that does not always lend itself to some rigid underlying theoretical framework. Rhetorical training itself tried to give an account of this complexity, when it specified that in addition to a main *status* each case could also present one or more *status incidentes*, which intervened in the treatment of secondary questions and could be different from the main one.[19] But such detailed subdivisions, even if they might have had some didactic utility, are usually abandoned in the practical development of a declamation.

In short, the impression we get from reading the anthologies is that the declamations, while originating as a useful exercise for the clarification and the teaching of a complex rhetorical theory, were eventually freed from the constraints of this theory and from this ancillary function—even if careful analysis can, here and there, still identify traces of this original didactic function of the different themes and the *status* they were called upon to illustrate and exemplify. But we have reached the moment of setting aside these aspects of the texts in order to try to understand who and what a Roman declamation speaks about.

---

16 Cf. Berti (2007), 116, n. 2.
17 Winterbottom (1988), 3.
18 Berti *per litteras*.
19 Cf. again Berti (2014), 134–137.

3

THEMES AND CHARACTERS

What is the subject matter of a Roman declamation? This question has no obvious easy answer, given the vast spectrum of situations, figures, and plots we find in the almost three hundred themes that have come down to us. And yet behind this variety it is still possible to identify certain recurrent themes—we may call them "hyperthemes" or "umbrella themes"—under which we can subsume a considerable portion of the available material. If, theoretically, any conflict could become the theme of a *controversia*, in the actual practice of the rhetorical schools some areas appear to have been greatly privileged.

In the first place, scholars have long recognized an outsize presence in the controversies of conflicts pertaining to the sphere of the family: a conspicuous number of themes depict frictions between fathers and sons, hostile or (conversely) incestuous relations between stepmothers and stepsons, even fatal encounters between brothers or husbands and wives. Yan Thomas, the great French scholar of Roman culture whose research represents some of the first systematic studies of the subject, counts in total 161 declamations involving family conflict, out of a total of 291 preserved texts.[1] If, generally speaking, the imaginary city of the declamations abounds in contrasts and disputes between its inhabitants, the nuclear family—the restricted environment of kinship—constitutes the focal point of this widespread conflict. As to the reasons for this situation, these have been identified as the desire to privilege situations that correspond to the real lives of the young apprentices, allowing them to verbalize frustrations and anxieties of retaliation and thus to experience a kind of escape valve for tensions inherent in the very structure of the Roman family. To examine the material systematically would require a book rather than a chapter! I will limit myself, then, to rapidly reviewing what tends to tear apart the "declamatory family", as it has been called by Elaine Fantham, and the frictions that most often emerge within it.[2]

---

[1] Thomas (1983), 125.
[2] Cf. Fantham (2004).

Themes and characters

Within declamation, as generally within all Roman culture, the prototypical family conflict, and focal point of all fault-lines that develop in familial relations, is that between fathers and sons.[3] There have even been those who have understood declamation as just one long reflection on notions of authority and paternity.[4] Conflict between fathers and sons normally emerges in the context of *abdicatio*, "disinheritance" or "disownment", which permitted a father to expel a child from the home on the basis of any infraction against him (shortly, we will have to clarify this quite vague expression). Such situations are so frequent in the school themes that many examples are ready at hand, as we can see already from the controversies of Seneca's first book given in Chapter 1: a father with three sons kills two of them in a fit of madness, then, when healed by the third son, the father disinherits him, because when he recuperates he recognizes his actions and realizes that the surviving son wants to take advantage of being his father's only remaining inheritor (*Minor* 256); a poor father disinherits his son when he marries the daughter of the father's wealthy enemy (in declamation, rich and poor are almost always in conflict), despite the fact that the girl's dowry has helped ransom the father from pirates (*Minor* 257); a father and a son both fight heroically, and when the law compels them fight in a duel for the title of most valorous, the father asks the son to give him the prize voluntarily, but the son refuses and is disinherited (*Minor* 258); under the same law, a rich man prohibits his son, a *vir fortis*, to fight in a duel against another hero who has previously killed two of the rich man's sons, and when the son refuses, he is disinherited by the father (*Minor* 271). And the list could easily go on and on.

Even from this brief survey of examples, disinheritance normally sanctions a son's behaviour when it does not conform to a father's wishes. Not coincidentally, one formulation of the declamatory law relating to *abdicatio*—not usually even mentioned in the theme, but simply assumed to be familiar to students—mentions the right to disinherit a son *minus dicto audientem*, "who does not obey".[5] In effect, the consistent claim of fathers in the world of school declamation is to be obeyed under any circumstance, regardless of the content of their commands—to the point that rhetoricians recommend dealing with a son's defence by preliminarily addressing the general question whether a son is obliged to do whatever his father orders him to do.[6] Fathers see themselves as

---

3 Cf. Thomas (1983); Sussman (1995); Vesley (2003); Fantham (2004); Lentano (2005); Breij (2006c) and (2015a), 14–40; Santorelli (2019).
4 Cf. Gunderson (2003).
5 Quintilian 7.1.14.
6 E.g., *Declamationes minores*, 271.1.

possessors of absolute power, above any law and countenancing no autonomous action at all by children:

> I, your father, have given you an order! This title is greater than any law. We throw down tribunes; we beat up candidates; to *us* has the right over life and death been given.[7]

In this perspective, the figure of the father, as normally represented in the school themes, appears to coincide with the cliché of the "severe father" who claims all the privileges that are recognized for him by custom and by law, and who takes advantage of these without concession or mediation. For a son to offer any resistance—including in cases where their private lives are involved, as in the many controversies where a father wishes to annul a son's marriage with some more economically promising match in mind—is an act of intolerable insubordination. In actual fact, severity and harshness are not the only characteristics attributed to the father figure in school rhetoric. Declamation features several fathers who are indulgent of their sons or who show solidarity with their sons' aspirations. However, these are definitely a minority of cases, and are often aimed at revealing other conflicts, such as between brothers. In this area, the influence of the traditional models appears very strong, and indeed overwhelming.[8]

This is not the place to rehash the decades-long debate about the exact nature of *abdicatio*, its analogies with the corresponding procedure of *apokéryxis* mentioned by Greek rhetoricians, and its relationship with the powers traditionally recognized for the *pater familias* or with principles attested in Roman law. In this respect, Quintilian's assertion that declamatory disinheritance has no exact parallel in the real world except—very approximately—in some cases argued before the centumviral tribunal, is, in my view, definitive.[9] "Approximately", because in Roman society disinheritance was stipulated through the will of a deceased person and thus could lead to accusations that the will was *inofficiosus*, whereas *abdicatio* takes place *inter vivos*, in the jurists' terminology, and its immediate effect seems to be not to exclude a son from inheritance so much as to estrange him from the domestic context and to disconnect him from the family. Thus, it seems more promising to attempt to understand what it means for declamation that disinheritance is so pervasive a theme.

---

7 *Declamationes maiores*, 6.14.6: pater iussi. Hoc nomen omni lege maius est: tribunos deducimus, candidatos ferimus, ius nobis vitae necisque concessum est. Cf. Lentano (2005).
8 Cf. Lentano in Brescia and Lentano (2009), 69–94.
9 Quintilian 7.4.11. Cf. Krapinger and Stramaglia (2015), 35–39.

Recent studies have seen in *abdicatio* an attenuated form of the Roman father's power over life and death, a sort of *ius vitae necisque* in miniature, which inflicts on the son a kind of civil death, but one that does not reach the level of an actual threat to his existence; or the formalization of a customary right recognized for the *pater familias* and occasionally evidenced in the sources, namely, of rejecting a child who has behaved incorrectly in the political sphere or in the family context.[10] Here I would like to suggest a further and different perspective from which to examine the question.

In the case mentioned earlier, and in many others, the son is disinherited not for behaviour that violates any law. In declamation, *abdicatio* is never represented as a family-level "duplicate" of some law that the city has inflicted or could inflict publicly upon a child. The distinction between the two levels is clarified by the declaimer Porcius Latro—the most authoritative figure among those cited in Seneca the Elder's collection—in response to the question whether it is legitimate to repudiate a son for actions he has taken legally:

> If [a son] has done something illegal, let the law mete out punishment. If he has done something legal but inopportune, let his father do so. Disinheritance does not relate to the commission of a crime, but to the shirking of responsibilities.[11]

It is hard to imagine a more Roman distinction than this, as it invokes the complex, multilayered concept of *officium*. Repudiation of a child does not pretend to be a substitute for civil law; nor does it represent itself as a private, familial version of the law. Instead, the two interventions exist on different planes, designated by Latro through the opposition between *licet* and *oportet* and between *scelus* and *officium*. The two pairings of terms are in fact closely related, as suggested by the definition of *oportet* that, internal to Roman culture itself, comes from Cicero's *Orator*, a text chronologically very close to Latro's. In Cicero, *oportere* is described as "the perfect completion of *officium*, which is equal for all and in all circumstances", in contradistinction to *decere*, which indicates a congruity between the individual and his or her behaviours and thus varies from person to person.[12] With *oportet*, then, Latro refers to what a son is called upon to do qua son, in the abstract role he plays within the family, regardless

---

10 Cf., most recently, Lentano (2014b), 46 ff., with bibliography; to this add the interesting contribution of Sciortino (2003).
11 Seneca, *Controversiae*, 10.2.8: si quid fecerit, quod non licet, lex vindicabit; si quid, quod licet, sed non oportet, pater. Non quaeritur de scelere filii, sed de officio.
12 Cicero, *Orator*, 74: oportere enim perfectionem declarat offici, quo et semper utendum est et omnibus, decere quasi aptum esse consentaneumque tempori et personae.

of the particular case envisioned in the theme of the controversy. At stake is what anthropologists call "attitudinal relations", behaviours that are culturally expected by one member of the group (in this case the nuclear family) towards the other members of the same group. As for *officium*, this is a term that escapes easy definition. The English word *duty* renders one of its many senses, but more precisely *officium* signifies full conformity with one's role, and in particular one's social role, and obligations an individual is expected to fulfil by virtue of the relationships that bind him to other members of the family and society. In other words, a son's *officium* coincides with the expression of *pietas*—another exquisitely Roman concept—with which it is often associated and of which it represents the behavioural manifestation.

We cannot ignore another implication of what Latro has said. Obeying the law is not sufficient for a son: this does not exhaust the totality of *officia* expected of him. In fact, there exist certain legally permissible behaviours that, nevertheless, are deemed unacceptable on the level of interpersonal relationships—at least by the demanding fathers of Latin declamation. In this sense, the father in Pseudo-Quintilian was not wrong to consider the very name of "father" to be *omni lege maius*, and the dozens of controversies on the subject of *abdicatio* can be read as a continuous reflection on the forms, limits, and substance of that "adaptation to role" to which terms such as *oportet* and *officium* make reference. They relentlessly discuss the duties of a child, negotiating the boundaries of autonomy and independence and questioning a category that is constitutively open, like that of "opportunity". At the same time, the father's power—far from given—becomes a problem, a claim that must be justified time and again before the virtual tribunal to which the parties present their respective cases. There are certainly cases in declamation where a repudiated son accepts unquestioningly whatever punitive measures have been levelled against him (the verb used in this case is usually *tacere*, as in the theme of Seneca 1.1); but usually the *abdicatus* challenges the father's decision and takes him to court, submitting this decision to the consideration of a third, impartial party. This solution is highly productive, insofar as it offers a pretext for examining the conflict between father and son from every possible angle.

Ritualized largely in the form of litigation in court, the father–son conflict in some cases reaches a level of hostility that even risks lives. In school themes, the father's right over life and death is often evoked but normally remains in the background, and is substituted by the more anodyne and contractual *abdicatio*. However, there are many themes in which a father does actually demand the death of a child, or at any rate would like to reach that point.[13] By the same

---

13 Twenty-two cases in total, according to Breij (2006c), now updated in Breij (2015a), 18–26.

token, there are many themes in which the son is accused of attempted patricide. Such an accusation can lead to a court trial, on the basis of *actio parricidii*, but also to a domestic trial that sometimes ends with a death sentence, as in Seneca the Elder's *Controversia* 7.1.[14] An obsession with patricide dominates the Roman cultural imagination, and it is no surprise that the rhetorical schools incorporate this theme as well. Declamations on the subject express the fear that the conflict between fathers and sons may reach such a point of hostility that it will overwhelm all "institutional" forms of conflict resolution envisioned in the City of the sophists, plunging the family into primordial, hopeless chaos.

Conflicts between fathers and sons do not, however, exhaust the range of controversies that feature members of the nuclear family as protagonists, even if they are the predominant form. Mention must also be made of those other members of the family who appear in the controversies, beginning with the figure of the mother.

In declamation, the mother is not normally a source of tension, except when she represents the second pole in the negotiation between opposing loyalties—the first being represented by the father (or sometimes, as in the sixteenth *Maior* of Pseudo-Quintilian, by a deserving friend). This is the case of Seneca's *Controversia* 1.4, in which a son must choose whether to kill his mother, who has been caught in the act of adultery, according to his father's demands, or instead hear her pleas of piety and spare her.[15] Or, again in Seneca, in *Controversia* 7.4, where ransoming the father captured by pirates is weighted against assisting the mother, who has become blind from grief at his absence. In general, relationships with the mother are characterized by solidarity and affection, in line with the ways in which this relationship is figured in Roman culture in the Republican period, very different from the rigidly formal relationship that characterizes interactions with the father. If, in this last respect, controversies about (suspicion of) patricide appear to be the extreme manifestation of a relationship that is nevertheless marked by an endemic conflict, in the case of the strongly affectionate relationship with the mother its extreme version is represented by the (suspicion of) incest, that unacceptable manifestation of an "excess of proximity" that may even justify the killing of the son, as happens in the last two *Maiores* of Pseudo-Quintilian.[16]

---

14 Cf. recently Rizzelli (2016); Rizzelli (2017), 26–31 and 35–43; for a complete survey of themes of patricide, see Lentano (2015b).
15 Cf. Casamento (2004a and 2013).
16 A recent study of incest in Roman declamation in Breij (2009); cf. now in Breij (2015a), 50–59.

Brothers, too, often appear in declamation in affectionate relationships, joined in opposition to the father.[17] In many controversies, for example, the conflict arises when the son has to choose whether to help his brother or his father: the twinned *Minores* 287 and 375 are of this type, and portray a *vir fortis* who has acted heroically in war, and who thus has the right to choose any prize, having to decide whether to save his brother (guilty of desertion and awaiting the death penalty) or his father (accused of treason). Choosing to save his brother—and thus only being able to assist his father at trial—this man is then disinherited after his father is judged innocent. They are exemplary because they demonstrate how the father–son relationship creates tensions with the son's other possible loyalties within the family. Here, disinheritance works to sanction not so much the son's refusal to ask for his father's pardon as his choice to privilege a horizontal sibling relationship, between equals, while spurning the fundamental bond that is represented by the father–son relationship (375.5):

> There are some situations, judges, that take on a different appearance when compared to others. The death of a brother is terrible in itself. But when compared to the risk of my own death, even this eventuality becomes acceptable.[18]

Direct conflict between brothers is relatively rare in the school themes (and conflict between sisters is practically absent). In the few examples that do exist, this conflict features what I have called elsewhere a "short circuit" of sharing. Almost mirror images of one another, joined from infancy by a common history and bound by a relation of strong reciprocal solidarity, and affection, brothers clash in declamation either when they aspire to a good that by its nature cannot be shared (e.g., the fiancée or the wife of the other brother, as in *Minores* 286 and 291) or, vice versa, when they wish to enjoy their inheritance exclusively, when this should instead be shared.

Continuing our analysis of the family in declamation, a few words are sufficient for the figure of the stepmother, probably the most stylized character in the universe of Sophistopolis.[19] The stepmother figures almost invariably as the enemy of children of the husband's first marriage, often for murky reasons relating to inheritance. Recent studies also underscore the character of the *virago*, the woman

---

17 Cf. Lentano in Brescia and Lentano (2009), 95–132.
18 375.5: Quaedam, iudices, comparatio minuit: per se crudele fuit perire fratrem, sed comparatum mihi tolerabile.
19 Cf. van Mal-Maeder (2007), 128–136; Brescia in Brescia and Lentano (2009), 145–179; Casamento (2015a); Pingoud and Rolle (2016); Valenzano (2016).

capable of an almost manly audacity who is willing to commit any crime.[20] In some cases, the stepmother and stepson are instead suspected of having a relationship that Roman culture considers incestuous, even in the absence of a blood relation between the partners. Whether overly hostile towards *privigni* or bound to them by relations of excessive closeness, the *noverca* is thus always positioned beyond cultural norms. In the few cases where we find "good" stepmothers (as in *Minor* 327), this reconfiguration can be explained by declamation's tendency to play with its own stereotypes or to introduce seemingly impossible themes, which require students to display great creativity and talent in defending a figure that appears almost automatically condemned by virtue of its role.

The literariness of depictions of stepmothers is indisputable. However, even if depictions of stepmothers accurately capture some pathology of the Roman *familia*—where the ease of divorce, very high infant mortality, and frequency of second marriages would have made the relationship with a stepmother a common experience for a significant number of adolescents—we must explore not only the historical plausibility of a figure of the declamatory universe, but also its functionality—that is, the role it plays in the narrative syntax of that universe and the way in which it contributes to its functioning.[21] Whereas the father figure appears to lend itself to the twinned representations of the severe, cruel father and of the indulgent father (and there are cases in which this figure shifts from one to the other), the figure of the mother presents very little variability, closely tied as it is to the cliché of closeness and solidarity with the requests of her children. The *noverca* therefore occupies the gap in this system, construed in declamation as a sort of anti-mother, a mirror image of the maternal figure, capable of taking on those traits of distance, aversion, or even open hostility. Not by chance, in those rare cases where a mother is defined as *crudelis*, the declaimer hastens to observe that her behaviour would be more appropriate to a *noverca*.[22]

If the *noverca* is almost always an anti-mother, she often also assumes the traits of an anti-wife, bound to the husband by murky hereditary aspirations rather than by attachment and dedication. Normally, the matrimonial bond appears in declamation to trump other and potentially coexisting family loyalties. Thus, in Seneca's *Controversia* 2.2, the wife does not want to break off her marriage, despite her father's command and in the presence of her husband's very questionable behaviour. In *Controversia* 2.5, the wife resists the torture inflicted on her by the tyrant without betraying her husband, who is involved in a plot to overthrow

---

20 Pingoud and Rolle (2016), 148-157.
21 Cf., among others, Vesley (2003), 162-166.
22 This is the case of the sixth *Maior* studied recently by Pingoud and Rolle (2016), 158-165; and think of Medea, a mother "fiercer even than a stepmother" in Ovid, *Heroides*, 6.127.

the despot. In 6.4, the wife wishes to commit suicide so to not outlive her husband, who has been proscribed. In 10.3, during the trauma of the civil war, the wife chooses to follow her spouse instead of her father, who is on the opposing side. In Pseudo-Quintilian's *Minor* 357, the wife refuses to abandon her husband despite his condemnation to blindness for adultery and her repudiation by her father; and so on.[23] If there is anything that can break this exceedingly strong bond, it is a husband who in some way compromises the safety of his children, whose side the mother then takes without hesitation, as we will see later.

But the mother who is loyal to the point of self-sacrifice is not the only possible manifestation of the conjugal relationship found in Roman declamation. In a culture marked by fear of female adultery and by the possible "contamination" of the blood(line), school rhetoric frequently confronts this theme and indeed develops it in many forms.[24] Controversies on this topic (in total, about 30 cases of the almost 300 surviving themes) can also involve conflicts between fathers and sons, as in Seneca's 1.4, where the son is disinherited for not having executed the two lovers, in spite of his father's orders. But mostly these turn on questions of the just exercise of the betrayed husband's right to kill, which is given to him by scholastic laws, just as the controversies on *abdicatio* relate to limitations on that paternal prerogative. The rhetoricians use all their creativity to invent situations that put the *ius occidendi* in conflict with the different specific cases in which it is applied: the husband who has killed the two lovers is in exile, and thus deprived of civil rights (*Minor* 244); the adulterous woman is pregnant and this gives her the right to have her execution delayed until she gives birth, a right that the betrayed husband has not respected (*Minor* 277); the wife believes *rumores* that her husband has died during a voyage and remarries, only to be surprised by him on his return, and killed together with her new partner (*Minor* 347); adultery is committed with an ex-fiancé or an ex-husband from whom the woman has been forced to separate, and this puts in question the legitimacy of the killing because "adultery" may not apply (*Minores* 286 and 291); and so on.

Adulterous conduct as such is never problematized. In this respect, declamation does not waver in its commitment to the traditional model of the female and to its corresponding sexual ethics. Not by chance, adultery is one of the few crimes in Sophistopolis that do not come under the jurisdiction of the courts (unless it involves an accusation *ex suspicione*, as in Seneca's *Controversia* 2.7, where there are clues but not clear evidence that the betrayal has actually been consummated, or in *Minor* 330; the juridical premise of *Minor* 300, where the adulterous woman

---

23 On the theme of conjugal love in declamation, see Mastrorosa (2002).
24 Cf. Brescia (2015a); Brescia and Lentano (2016); Lentano (2016a); Valenzano (2019).

Themes and characters

is brought to trial first in a domestic court, and a second time in the Forum, is not clear). In a world where almost all conflicts end up in court, the repression of female conduct remains the prerogative of her husband, and if he is brought to court, it is only when there is some doubt whether he has abused the prerogatives recognized for him by law. Even in this case, however, there is a distinction. The inviolability of marriage remains a non-negotiable value, as often reiterated (e.g., in *Minor* 249.19), but students familiarized themselves with the idea that many circumstances could intervene to limit the husband's punitive powers and even to make the woman's behaviour justifiable in some way, as in the *Minores* 286 and 291.

We opened this series of examples by observing that family conflicts represent a significant portion of the themes proposed by teachers to their students. But naturally these do not exhaust the possible questions dealt with by the school themes. So what else does Roman declamation deal with?

The second most frequent topic in the preserved material relates to what we could call the allocation of wealth. In some cases, the two motifs are actually tightly interwoven, as for example in the controversies that see two brothers fighting over inheritance or sons accused of attempted patricide. Almost invariably, fathers who make this accusation attribute their sons' presumed homicidal intentions to uncontainable greed, to the desire of getting their hands on their father's coveted wealth (thus, e.g., in *Minor* 258.9). The charge of being *luxuriosus* and so of privileging hedonistic consumption over virtuous accumulation can be brought both against fathers (who then become accused of insanity by their sons, as in the theme of Seneca 2.6) and against sons (who then run the risk of being disinherited, as in Seneca 3.3). In each case, the behaviour is strongly censured, especially if enacted by someone who should act as guarantor of culturally accepted models for the use of goods.[25]

In Sallust's time, and before that in the period of Cato the Elder, *luxuria* was a sign of a perverted relationship with wealth. The exemplary biographical trajectory, which a father could claim with the pride of one who knows he has conformed fully with traditional models, is that depicted in *Minor* 316: "From young adulthood, I led a frugal life. I increased my patrimony. I married. I raised a son".[26] This can be compared with Terence's portrait of the *pater severus* Demea, co-protagonist of the *Adelphoe*: "he lived always saving and working, took a wife, and brought two sons into the world".[27] Limiting self-indulgent consumption, conserving and increasing the inherited patrimony, fulfilment of the "civic" obligation of marriage and producing children, continued to be the cornerstones

---

25 On *controversia* 2.6 cf. now Bianco (2018).
26 316.5: Iuvenis frugaliter vixi, patrimonium auxi, uxorem duxi, filium sustuli.
27 45–47: semper parce ac duriter / se habere; uxorem duxit; nati filii / duo.

of the only ethics of wealth that Roman culture was capable of elaborating over the course of its history.

The overlap between family conflict and questions relating to the distribution of wealth would be much greater, if those who believe *abdicatio* entailed disinheritance along with disownment are right. This is certainly true in the case of Greek *apokéryxis*. For the world of Latin declamation, the question is controversial, not least because it is a question that did not particularly energize the rhetoricians, except in cases where the theme involved the death of the father and so required clarification of the hereditary position of the *abdicatus* (as happens, e.g., in *Minor* 374). But conflicts relating to access to wealth are also placed outside the family.

To this category belong the numerous *controversiae* centring on enmity between a rich man and a poor man.[28] This theme was so common that in Petronius's *Satyricon*, when Trimalchio invites the rhetorician Agamemnon to propose a theme of declamation, he begins with the words *Pauper et dives inimici erant*, only to be immediately interrupted by the host, who in his arrogance claims not to know the meaning of *pauper*.[29] In such a genre as *controversia*, which is based on conflict, the opposition between wealth and poverty represents a very convenient departure point, a situation in which hostility appears to be already inherent, with no need of any pretext to be translated into action. However, it has been observed that this opposition is not particularly unexpected in the context of imperial Rome—in a reality, that is, where social inequalities were progressively radicalized and where they would soon be codified in the odious legal distinction between *honestiores* and *humiliores*, roughly coinciding with the opposition between wealthy élites and the subaltern classes.[30]

The political-ideological matrix of the rich/poor opposition appears to characterize Greek declamation especially, where it probably reflects the deep mistrust of wealth lodged in the Athenian cultural imagination, which saw in the wealthy so many potential adversaries of the democratic system. Thus, it is in Greek declamation (as exemplified, e.g., in the *De statibus* of Hermogenes 3.19 Patillon = 49, 20–22 Rabe) that the young man accused of aspiring to tyranny is qualified as "rich", where instead Pseudo-Quintilian's *Minor* 267, which translates this theme into Latin, speaks generically of "some such man".[31] In the Roman

---

28 Examined recently by Santorelli (2014), 16–24 and now Breij (2016), 276–278, who counts more than thirty apposite themes, and Breij (2020), 13–32.
29 Petronius 48.
30 Cf. Migliario (1989).
31 Qui tyrannidem deposuerat sub pacto abolitionis iuxta arcem flens deprehensus est. Adfectatae tyrannidis reus est.

context, economic disparity alone appears sufficient to arouse class hatred, with all its implications for prestige and influence on one hand and lack of social capital on the other. More than once, the court seems to represent a level playing field, offering even to the weakest members of society the possibility of having their voices heard and of escaping conflict through negotiation, rejecting the logic of feuds.

Besides the conventional conflict between *dives* and *pauper*, less stereotyped themes relating to the domain of wealth are found frequently, especially in the *Minores*: for example, the inheritance of a *raptor* contested by his relatives and the *rapta* who *in articulo mortis* decides to marry him; distribution of wealth is imposed by law on all citizens to avoid the emergence of tyranny; restitution of deposits; dispositions of wills in favour of friends and freedmen; goods confiscated by the city and whose restitution is petitioned; the inheritance of a sacrilegious assassin contested between the temple and the accuser; gifts offered by patrons and refused by their clients; cancellation of debts and their effects on a will that has two brothers as its beneficiaries; disposition of goods undeclared to the tax authorities; the inheritance of an archpirate claimed by the slave girl who a father has offered to him to marry instead of his daughter; accusations relating to the economic exploitation of guardianship; fights between mothers-in-law and daughters-in-law, both widowed, over their dowries; charges brought by pimps who have seen their money squandered after one of their girls has taken a love potion offered by her lover; and so on. Among other things, it is no coincidence that the only Roman law explicitly mentioned as such in declamation (*Minor* 264) has to do with questions precisely of a patrimonial nature: this is the so-called *Lex Voconia* (actually a plebiscite passed in 169 BCE by the tribune Quintus Voconius Saxa)–controversial in principle, probably quickly avoided and eventually set aside, but which in any case limited the hereditary rights of women, apparently to avoid excessive concentrations of wealth.[32]

I do not know of a parallel in Greek declamation. In any case, the presence of economic themes in Latin school rhetoric has not been exhaustively studied.[33] And yet it captures a profound characteristic of Roman culture and society, where legislation regarding wealth, honourable forms of acquiring it, limits on its consumption, its protection of the existing social order, and above all on its hereditary transmission (wills, legacies, trusts, donations, adoptions, and so on) already from the period of Twelve Tables had a huge role to play in legal regulation. Declamation faithfully reflects its legislative and cultural centrality.

---

32 Cf. Bettinazzi (2014), 9–34; Lentano (2014b), 104–107; Mantovani (2014). On the law see now McClintock (2022).
33 Cf. Santorelli (2016a).

Introducing Roman Declamation

In many cases, declamation depicts situations that could actually take place in real life and addresses these situations using models that were not dissimilar to those used "in the field" by jurists. From this point of view, it is relevant that the *controversiae* in which Romanists have tended to see analogies with the arguments of classical jurisprudence are precisely those that belong to the category we are examining. More generally, school rhetoric demonstrates that it fully understood the importance that questions and conflicts tied to the preservation and to the transmission of wealth had in Roman culture, and that it gave them an appropriate amount of treatment within the training it offered to its "users", who all came from an elite whose main privilege was property ownership.

In the family and in the many conflicts arising therein, as well as in the circulation of wealth (with all the possible intersections between these contexts), Roman declamation identified the two great problematic nodes for constructing its stories. Before closing this survey of themes and figures in the universe of school rhetoric, however, we need to mention certain other characters who had special status within declamation. As should be obvious, the universe of Sophistopolis is highly litigious. It is also regulated, if nothing else by virtue of the fact that the possibility of bringing illegal behaviours to justice was guaranteed to all its inhabitants, thanks to its articulated system of laws. But beyond the walls of the tidy City of the sophists there is also a space of disorder, of danger, and of subversion of cultural rules. This is a space—mostly marine, sometimes terrestrial—that in declamation is indicated normally through the adverb *peregre*. Those who inhabit it or come from it are often possessors of potentially disruptive Otherness, which must be guarded against and with which relations of reciprocity and exchange are impossible. Therefore, as in the corpus of the stories of magic studied by Vladimir Propp in the famous *Morphology of the Folktale*, distance from "home" in declamation often triggers successive developments of events, either because foreign contact acts as the harbinger of injury or because the absence of the husband presages an onset of changes that will need to be taken account of on return.[34]

This is the case for Seneca the Elder's *Controversia* 2.7, which we have already cited for the accusation of adultery brought *ex suspicione* (and in similar terms, by Pseudo-Quintilian's *Minor* 363):

> A man who had a beautiful wife departed for a foreign country. A foreign merchant moved into the neighbourhood. He propositioned the man's wife three times for adultery, promising monetary compensation; she refused. The merchant died, and in his will left the beautiful woman as inheritor of all

---

34 Imber (2008) has recently insisted on this point. Cf. also Nocchi (2017 and 2018).

his goods and added a note of praise: "I found a loyal woman". The woman accepted the inheritance. Her husband returns and accuses her of adultery on suspicion.[35]

Ancient culture naturally did not have to wait for declamation before elaborating negative images of merchants, whose itinerancy afforded an easy metaphor for ethical untrustworthiness and whose persuasive and tricky speech could be deployed both to hawk wares and to entice defenceless matrons into adulterous affairs. In our case, the departure of the husband towards *peregre* and the arrival of the presumptive seducer constitutes an inversion of internal and external, whereby the chaos that pertains to the latter comes to be in the very heart of the cultural cosmos, threatening it up close. The problematic outcome of this encounter is already inscribed in this topological inversion.

The figure of the merchant appears very rarely in the extant declamations. By contrast, the figure of the pirate is a fixed inhabitant of the world external to Sophistopolis, not subject to the *negotiator*'s mobility.[36] Inheriting a characterization of pirates long established in the Greek imaginary, in Roman declamation the figure of the pirate is marked above all by his foreignness to culture in every form—from his addiction to blood to his barbarism, from his systematic infringement of the law to his generalized exercise of violence. Even the pirate's physical appearance is portrayed as going beyond the norm in terms of colour of his skin, the dimensions of his body, the shade of his hair, the ferocity of his gaze, and more. To offer only one example, in the depiction given by Cestius Pius, pirates are "disposed to every cruelty; they make sport of legal and illegal; undertake thievery on land and on sea; they take other goods at sword-point; their outward appearance reflects their cruelty and their addiction to human blood, and they flaunt laces and chains". Moreover, they are naturally inclined to imprison any unfortunate soul that happens to fall into their hands, and to threaten the honour of chaste matrons and pure virgins.[37]

---

35 Quidam, cum haberet formosam uxorem, peregre profectus est. In viciniam mulieris peregrinus mercator commigravit. Ter illam appellavit de stupro adiectis pretiis; negavit illa. Decessit mercator, testamento heredem omnibus bonis reliquit formosam et adiecit elogium: "Pudicam repperi". Adit hereditatem. Redit maritus, accusat adulteri ex suspicione. A vast amount of scholarship is available on this *controversia*, including Lentano (1998), 105–129; Berti (2007), 43–78; Rizzelli (2011).
36 For what follows I draw on Lentano (2018a), to which I refer the reader also for a rich bibliography.
37 Seneca, *Controversiae*, 1.2.8: Non est credibile temperasse a libidine piratas omni crudelitate efferatos, quibus omne fas nefasque lusus est, simul terras et maria latrocinantes, quibus in aliena impetus per arma est; iam ipsa fronte crudeles et humano sanguine adsuetos, praeferentes ante se vincula et catenas.

These traits are inherited from an extensive literary tradition and are constantly varied by declaimers. Besides individual episodes featuring pirates as protagonists, in the school themes the pirate represents the Other par excellence, unassimilable, a source of disorder that cannot be accommodated and that resists any attempt at acculturation or regulation. The society to which the pirate belongs is the reverse of the city and the opposite of the world in which and to which the rhetoricians trained the young aristocrats who attended their schools. Not coincidentally, pirates never appear, *nisi fallor*, as a counterpart in debates imagined taking place in court. By definition, pirates cannot tolerate having their motives discussed in such an exquisitely "civil" context. In this sense, pirates are like another figure systematically excluded from forensic contexts, namely the tyrant—a sort of "internal Other", a malignant presence in the otherwise healthy body of the city. It is worthwhile tarrying briefly on this figure.

The declamations relating to tyrants and tyrannicides have already been discussed in the excellent and irreplaceable monograph of Raffaella Tabacco, published nearly forty years ago.[38] Tabacco has demonstrated that the figure of the tyrant is very strongly stereotyped and characterized above all by simple-minded and arbitrary ferocity; morbid suspiciousness; an absence of relations with the rest of the civic body; jealous physical, and psychological closeness; solitariness in the well-protected precinct of the citadel; and so on. Naturally, declamation did not invent these traits, but adopted and adapted them from an established tradition going back to Greek (and in particular Athenian) political thought. The tyrant of school rhetoric represents, moreover, a negation of the values on which a well-regulated society is based: he tortures free men, violating a fundamental norm in declamation (Seneca, *Controversia* 2.5, where the victim is also a woman);[39] he issues proclamations ordering sons to behead their fathers, according to a theme referenced by Petronius in the opening of the *Satyricon* and an exact parallel of which has been found in Greek;[40] or he forces sons to beat their fathers, whereas a standard law of *controversiae* says that for such behaviour a son's hands should be cut off (Seneca, *Controversia* 9.4); and he authorizes slaves to kill their masters and to rape their mistresses, inverting the social order and vicariously exhibiting the predatory and voracious sexuality that is typical of the tyrant in the Greek imaginary (Seneca, *Controversia* 7.6).

---

38 Tabacco (1985); I refer readers to the fifth chapter for the question of possible political meanings of the theme. On tyrants (and tyrannicides) in declamation see also Schwartz (2016); Casamento (2018); Enrico (2021).

39 Cf. Pagán (2007–08); bibliography on torture in Roman declamation includes also Bernstein (2012); Zinsmaier (2015); Papakonstantinou (2017); Breij (2020), 32–51; Breij (2021).

40 Stramaglia (2015), 148–150.

The hero of declamation is the tyrannicide—the only figure, together with the *vir fortis*, to whom school laws give absolute discretion in choosing a prize for a meritorious act. And naturally, declamatory jurisprudence recognizes the crime of *adfectatio tyrannidis*—an act so grave that it justifies even patricide (as in *Minor* 322)—and is suspicious of any behaviour that smacks of tyranny, as when a man is accused of aspiring to absolute power simply because he was unable to gaze upon the citadel (the tyrant's typical abode, metonymic of tyranny itself) without shedding a tear (*Minor* 267).[41]

Pirates do not appear in declamation as an excuse for speaking about maritime security or of conflicts between irreconcilable worlds. Similarly, tyranny is never realized in action in Sophistopolis. It is something that happens elsewhere, or in the past, or is a dangerous aspiration that must be guarded against.[42] Almost always, the appearance of pirates or tyrants is simply the trigger of a conflict that belongs to the sphere of the family—because a father hesitates to ransom his son and the stepmother intervenes; because a son has to abandon his blind mother to reach his father; because a father can only afford to ransom one of his two sons who have been captured by pirates; because a son kills his father for *adfectatio tyrannidis* only then to be suspected of aspiring to tyranny himself; or because after killing two tyrant sons, a father demands as his reward that his third be sent into exile; and so on. The appearance of these figures thus functions to generate tensions within the universe of family relations, provoking conflicts or exposing the members of that universe to complex choices. Even when declamation sets its sights on the vast seas and the risks of journeys, the secrets of power or dark aspirations for despotism, it always ends up bringing this back within the walls of the home and the boundaries of the family, as if evoking the Other and Elsewhere is only the umpteenth pretext for talking about the Self.

---

41 See Nocchi (2019).
42 See Tabacco (1985), 9–14.

4

CULTURE IN DECLAMATION

"In public, a father followed his *luxuriosus* son, crying. He is accused of *dementia*." This is the theme of Pseudo-Quintilian's *Minor* 316, a controversy that has been examined within a recent study of the meaning of *dementia* in school rhetoric and its connection to juridical reflection.[1] And, indeed, the *Sermo*—that is, the sort of commentary that often accompanies or is interspersed in the text of a declamation, or even is substituted for it—lingers on this point. But I would like to draw the reader's attention to the following passage, where we seem to hear the voice of the teacher as he speaks to his students in a lesson:

> I do not want someone to criticize me because I do not give you space for practising *loci communes*. If you want to expand declamation and use your creativity, you can add elements that do not relate in any way to the case at hand, but that perhaps contribute to the audience's enjoyment.[2]

The text continues, in the voice of the accused father:

> I have not yet provided specific personal reasons for my tears. But who should be surprised that a grown man weeps? Infancy begins from tears and often fate puts us in the condition of crying. What day does not present us with something sad and woeful? Even if every other reason for crying is lacking, the sight of other men and consideration of our morality are sufficient to provoke tears. Relations of friendship and of family, encounters, feelings and successes, all in a short space of time come to nothing and slip away. And what day passes without seeing a funeral?[3]

---

1 Flens pater per publicum filium luxuriosum sequebatur. Dementiae reus est. Cf. Rizzelli (2014b).
2 316.7: Nolo quisquam me reprehendat tamquam vobis locos non dem. Si ampliare declamationem voletis et ingenium exercere, dicetis quod ad causam huius nullo modo, ad delectationem aurium fortasse pertineat.
3 316.8-9: Nondum privatas ac peculiares lacrimarum reddo causas; interim, quis miratur flere hominem? Hinc infantia incipit, in hanc necessitatem plerumque fortuna deducit. Quis enim est dies qui non triste aliquid et flebile nobis minetur? Si nullam aliam rationem lacrimarum haberemus, conspectus tamen hominum et ratio mortalitatis poterat elicere fletus. Hae amicitiae, hae propinquitates, hi congressus, haec studia laudesque intra breve temporis momentum occident atque labentur. Quotus quisque transit dies quo non funus accipiamus?

Reflections like this are a good example of the philosophical colouring that often tinges Latin declamation and represents a point of contact with other texts that precede the period of Quintilian. For example, the *topos* of human life that begins from weeping—which extends at its far chronological end to Leopardi in his *Canto notturno*—can be found in Lucretius and Pliny the Elder, in the opening of his book on Man, while the image of daily funerals that remind us of the precarity of the human condition pervades Seneca's *Consolatio ad Marciam*.[4]

The relation of school rhetoric to philosophy is a field of research that remains only partially explored by scholars and is certainly promising. Positions such as that of Charles Guérin, according to whom declamation casts philosophical discourse as completely foreign to its interests, or even likely to harm the literary pleasure that comes with the practice of controversy, do not seem to be substantiated by detailed analysis.[5] Indeed, philosophical digressions are presented by Pseudo-Quintilian as capable of increasing the audience's *delectatio*. After Michael Winterbottom's discussion of the subject, important studies have been produced by Andrea Balbo on Calpurnius Flaccus, by Lucia Pasetti in reference both to the *Declamationes Minores* and to the *Maiores*, a collection that in its extent and high level of literary refinement lends itself to such a study, and most recently by Gernot Krapinger and Thomas Zinsmaier.[6] Recurrent motifs include the question of divine providence and (closely connected) that of the value of divination, and more generally of the entire apparatus of oracles, predications, spells, and wonders that pertain to the field of the "fantastic" in declamation. Also lending themselves to philosophical reflection are those controversies in which an aspiring suicide, in homage to principles of scholastic jurisprudence, argues his reasons to the Senate under penalty of being denied burial. In this respect, we can identify in Pseudo-Quintilian's material numerous points of contact with texts of Seneca. The two themes converge in the fourth *Maior*, *The Astrologer*, where the defence of the providentiality of the world and of the credibility of divination is used to justify a *vir fortis*'s request to commit suicide after the *mathematicus* who appears in the title of the declamation has prophesied that he will kill his father:

> What then of this awesome spectacle of the brilliant stars? Some shine as though they are fixed to the sky and of a piece with it, in unchanging positions that they have taken up once for all, while others, scattered all over the heavens,

---

4 Cf. respectively Lucretius, 5.226–227; Pliny the Elder, 7.2; Seneca, *Consolatio ad Marciam*, 9.2.
5 Guérin (2012–13), 27.
6 Cf. Balbo (2019); Winterbottom (2006); Pasetti (2007, 2008, 2009, and 2016); Krapinger and Zinsmaier (2021).

trace out wandering courses, erratic yet predetermined. Do you imagine all these things were set in order at random or by chance? I ask you, how could reason have done any better? God, yes, god, the maker of the whole immeasurable structure, drew these things forth from that primordial shapeless darkness and gave them an appearance, dividing them up into parts.[7]

Here, the appeal to reason as the ordering principle of the universe betrays the Stoic cast of Pseudo-Quintilian's work. And indeed Stoicism does dominate the philosophical landscape of school declamation.[8] By contrast, in the tenth *Maior*, where a son who has died *ante diem* continues to appear to his mother until his father has his tomb enchanted by a mage, Patrick Kragelund recognizes echoes of Epicurean philosophy, especially its attack on beliefs about the afterlife and its affirmation that the dead have no sensation and thus no possibility of enjoying the manifestations of grief.[9] Finally, Lucia Pasetti has called attention to controversies featuring the figure of the Cynic philosopher, especially *Minor* 283.[10] If adherents of this philosophical school are often subjected to aggression or derision in the Greek context, in Latin declamation themes appear in which Cynics are taken to task for choices that contradict Roman *mores*. There is also, generically, that traditional Roman indifference to purely speculative activity, expressly claimed as an identity trait in *Minor* 283. But in the case of Cynic philosophy, this argument is accompanied more specifically by an aversion to choices that deliberately flout dominant models of living and values.

All told, the case of Cynicism remains isolated. In the school controversies, explicit references to this or that teaching are in fact rare, and the positions of the declaimers do not seem to embody any specific system of thought. Philosophers, when they appear, are above all a mechanism for navigating out of the often narrow boundaries of some situations, as, for example, in Seneca's *Controversia* 7.6, about the father who has given his daughter in marriage to an ex-slave and who is thus accused of dementia by his son:

> Albucius also spoke philosophically. He said that no one is a slave and no one is free by nature, and that fate imposes these labels on each person.

---

[7] 4.13.5-4.14.1: *Quid haec fulgentium siderum veneranda facies? Quod quaedam velut infixa ac cohaerentia perpetua semelque capta sede conlucent, alia toto sparsa caelo vagos cursus certis emetiuntur erroribus, ista credis passim fortuitoque disposita? Rogo, quid melius ratio fecisset? Deus haec, deus, fabricator operis immensi, ex illa rudi primaque caligine protracta posuit in vultum, digessit in partes.*
[8] Pasetti (2016), 99. On the fourth *Maior* see also Krapinger and Zinsmaier (2021), 151–155.
[9] Kragelund (1991).
[10] Cf. Pasetti (2016).

"You know the rest", he added, "that we too were once slaves", and he recalled the case of Servius Tullius.[11]

The motif echoes a well-known Stoic principle, expressed by Seneca in a memorable formulation, but the trope occurs in declamations in relation to many different topics.[12] This is a *locus communis* in a technical sense, belonging to those standard argumentative formulations used by the rhetoricians, who drew on them like a reservoir in the most diverse circumstances, and owing their name to their adaptability, on subjects such as the mutability of fortune, contempt of death, the eternity of glory, condemnation of wealth, and praise for virtuous poverty. Hence, the often merciless judgements that have been pronounced on "declamatory philosophy": Antonio Stramaglia has actually spoken of "doctrinally superficial snippets of skill".[13]

I would like to suggest a different interpretation of such philosophical insertions into declamation, however. In the first place, they confirm school rhetoric as a genre that is capable of drawing on the most diverse expressions of culture. The *problémata philosophoúmena*, as Seneca the Elder called them (*Controversia* 1.3.8), belonged, very specifically, to a widespread patrimony of knowledge shared by the educated classes and, as such, expected to be learnt and deployed at opportune moments by speakers in training. Furthermore—and the point is closely related—these "snippets of skill" operated on a level we could call "meta-communicative", in the sense that they aim to reassure the consumers of the discourse that the orator and his audience speak the same language, share the same codes, and are joined by possession of the same cultural baggage. More than contributing to clarification of the controversy in question (in respect to which they often appear digressive), they provide information about the orator, contributing to his authoritative image and characterizing him as a member of the same educated *élite* to which the judges also belonged.

What is more, in Roman declamation there are examples of rhetoricians whose strong theoretical vocation eventually resulted in a decision to leave the classroom to take up philosophical speculation. This is the case of Papirius Fabianus, a diligent adherent of the schools and then a student of the philosopher Sestius and author of naturalistic and scientific texts.[14] As a declaimer, Papirius

---

11 7.6.18: Albucius et philosophatus est: dixit neminem natum liberum esse, neminem servum; haec postea nomina singulis imposuisse Fortuna. Denique, inquit, scis et nos nuper servos fuisse. Rettulit Servium regem.
12 Cf. Citti (2015a), 121–122 and notes.
13 Stramaglia (2013), 159.
14 All information on this figure in Migliario (2007), 29 and note 87 and now Huelsenbeck (2018), 65–152, both with extensive bibliography; evidence and fragments in Garbarino (2003), 126–136.

did not spurn the *loci communes* of traditional philosophy, which were then reprised by Seneca the Younger, such as the juxtaposition of Man's ferocity and that of animals (who are not aggressive with members of their own species). Among other things, this motif recurred in one of the many *controversiae* about *abdicatio*, Seneca the Elder's 2.1. The author of the *Declamationes minores* would have deemed it a typical example of philosophical elaboration aimed only at the pleasure of the audience.[15] Here, instead, is how Papirius expressed himself in the first Senecan *suasoria* to dissuade Alexander from navigating the encircling ocean:

> Those who have observed the movements of the stars and the alternation of winter and summer, attributing them to fixed laws, and who know every part of the universe, nevertheless are uncertain about the surrounding Ocean, if it encircles the lands like a belt or if it gathers in a circle and pours boiling—as if with immense breaths—in those loops in which navigation takes place, and whether beyond it there is a fire—which it nourishes—or air.[16]

It comes as no surprise that at least three books *On Natural Causes* were attributed to Fabianus.

Regarding the relation between declamation and the broader cultural imaginary, it is worth mentioning briefly another point only partially studied by scholars, that of declamation's connection to historiography.[17] As already clear from the examples given in the preceding chapters, *controversiae* and *suasoriae* do not necessarily involve fictitious situations or figures of myth. In some cases, they feature figures and events drawn from history—indeed, in Suetonius's judgement, this was a defining feature of Roman declamation in its most ancient form, whereas in Greece the presence of historical themes appears to be a later development.[18] In the early twentieth century, Richard Kohl has surveyed chronologically all the *argumenta ex historia petita* known to him; this catalogue is of immense utility but needs updating with the new texts that have

---

15 Complete analysis in Casamento (2002).
16 1.4: Illi, qui iam siderum collegerunt meatus et annuas hiemis atque aestatis vices ad certam legem redegerunt, quibus nulla pars ignota mundi est, de Oceano tamen dubitant, utrumne terras velut vinculum circumfluat en in suum colligatur orbem et in hos per quos navigatur sinus quasi spiramenta quaedam magnitudinis exaestuet; ignem post se, cuius alimentum ipse sit, habeat an spiritum. Cf. now Huelsenbeck (2020).
17 For the Greek world: Russell (1983), 106–128 and now Cribiore (2001), 231–244; Lupi (2010), 27–32 and above all Webb (2006); for Rome, summary in Nicolai (1992), 83–88; Nicolai (2008), esp. 160ff.; Citti (2015b), and most recently Traina (2021).
18 Thus Philostratus, *Vitae sophistarum*, 1; in Suetonius, *ex historiis* must mean "from historical events"; cf. Nicolai (1996), 84.

emerged from papyri.[19] Still, it emerges that historical themes are less represented in the Latin school than in the Greek context, where around 350 are known. And this small number is further reduced if the cases of Latin *controversiae* relating to figures of Greek history are discounted (a citizen of Olynthus, Iphicrates, the sculptor Phidias, and the painter Parrhasius, Cimon son of Miltiades, in Seneca, *Controversiae* 3.8, 6.5, 8.2, 9.1, 10.5; a guest of Olynthus, Alexander the Macedonian, Demosthenes, and again Iphicrates in Pseudo-Quintilian, *Declamationes minores* 292, 323, 339, 386).[20]

Themes from Roman history are scarce. Apart the themes relating to Cicero, we have a Senecan *controversia* on Lucius Caecilius Metellus and the rescue of the Palladium, referring to the episode of 251 BCE, and one on the episode of Lucius Quintius Flamininus who in 184 BCE, during a meal, had a prisoner executed for pleasing his mistress.[21] *Suasoriae* offer a confirmation in this sense: of the seven preserved by Seneca the Elder, only two relate to episodes of recent Roman history: the assassination of Cicero by Antony's henchman (also dealt with in Seneca's *Controversia* 7.2), while another two pairs relate to the deeds of Alexander of Macedon and those of the Persian Wars.[22]

Entirely different are those themes—exclusively in Seneca the Elder, which is already an important datum—in which some historical reference can be presumed, but only generically and without mentioning precise figures or events. Elvira Migliario has observed that at least three *controversiae* (4.8, 6.4, and 10.3) evoke a context of civil war and represent proscriptions; these were likely to have been created in the climate immediately following the excesses of the triumvirs, beginning at the end of 43 BCE.[23] What is more, the passages in question are situated after the end of the proscriptions and explore their aftermath and the social problems they bring, once the most acute phase had passed. Several decades later, such questions were perceived as undeniably outdated, which explains their absence in the collections of Pseudo-Quintilian and Calpurnius Flaccus.

It is not easy to account for the absence of historical themes in Roman declamation. Perhaps it comes down to perceptions of the cultural value of historiography in relation to school rhetoric; Seneca the Elder insists on this point (*Suasoria* 6.16). Or perhaps it is a fear that figures and situations crystallized in the annalistic tradition and congealed in the *exempla* tradition did not

---

19 Kohl (1915).
20 On Seneca 10.5 cf. Casamento (2016); on *Minor* 292 Pasetti (2018); Pingoud (2020), 167–179; on 323 Visonà (2021); on 339 van Mal-Maeder (2018a).
21 Cf. respectively 4.2 and 9.2. On the former theme cf. Casamento (2004b).
22 *Suasoriae* on Cicero have been often studied: cf. *inter alia* Borgo (2014).
23 Cf. Migliario (2009), 57.

give rhetoricians enough space to explore, constraining students within rigid boundaries. The difference between Greek and Roman declamation in this respect has been traced to the need to preserve and defend the cultural identity of Greece under the Roman empire, a demand that would have been much less relevant to Roman rhetoricians, for obvious reasons.[24] Much discussion has been devoted to the problem of how free declaimers felt to adapt historical episodes to their needs; in principle, the requirements of historicity would have put quite severe limits on creativity. In practice, declaimers do take liberties with history, even to the point of anachronism, and the manuals warn teachers against this. The historiographical tradition certainly imposed strict constraints: as has been observed for Greek rhetoric, a rhetorician could not make the Athenians winners of the expedition to Sicily or paint Critias as anything other than a tyrant. But within those limits, ample space existed for meaningful alteration, much as the tragedians often took license vis-à-vis mythical events.[25] But this is only one aspect of the problem. Declamatory rewriting of historical events not only entails the invention of fictitious circumstances or ad hoc addition of details, but more generally a process of re-adaptation that colours those events with features of the new literary code within which they have been adopted. Out of this emerge *argumenta* that are different from other subjects of controversy only because of their use of proper names or their mention of factual situations; but they could function equally without such details.

Seneca's *Controversia* 7.2, regarding the murder of Cicero, is a good example:

> *Legal action is permitted for bad behaviour.* Cicero defended and won the acquittal of Popillius, on charges of patricide. When Cicero was proscribed, Popillius, sent by Antony, killed him and took his head to Antony. He is accused of bad behaviour.[26]

As Emanuele Berti has observed, in the theme proposed to students "we could take out all the proper names, replace Antony with some anonymous *tyrannus*, substitute Cicero and Popillius with some generic pair of *patronus* and *cliens*, and obtain an equally coherent theme, consistent with other declamations in the Senecan corpus".[27] School rhetoric reveals, in short, a tendency to assimilate themes—whatever their origin—to its own conventions, and

---

24 Russell (1983), 107–108; Webb (2006), 27; Penella (2014).
25 Webb (2006), 29, and Russell (1983), 113–117.
26 DE MORIBUS SIT ACTIO. Popillium parricidii reum Cicero defendit; absolutus est. Proscriptum Ciceronem ab Antonio missus occidit Popillius et caput eius ad Antonium rettulit. Accusatur de moribus.
27 Berti (2007), 209.

conceptual and juridical frames. It does not hesitate to fabricate fictitious elements in order to make this assimilation more complete. Thus, in the case of the *controversia* on the death of Cicero, Seneca states that the declaimers imagined Popillius defended by his future victim against charges of patricide, where in fact Cicero had assisted him in a private case (7.2.8). There have even been some scholars who have doubted the very existence of an assassin named Popillius with this specific background of relations with his future victim.[28] More interesting is the fact that traces of this declamatory creation can be found in historiographical and biographical texts of the imperial period, evidently influenced by school rhetoric. So this influence is not limited to deforming and adapting figures and historical events, but extends even to giving those events a contour that appears in successive historiographical narratives. Similarly, in Seneca's *controversia* relating to Metellus, the *pontifex maximus* who was blinded after rescuing the statue of Athena from a fire—which only the Vestal Virgins had the right to approach—the blindness is in all likelihood an invention of the declaimers, who want the incident to interact with the general principle that a priest be physically whole. And yet in Pliny the Elder, some forty years after the publication of the Senecan anthology, this element is taken for granted as an established historical truth (7.141). Just like the relation between declamation and literature, that between declamation and historiography is a two-way street.

In Chapter 6, we return to historical *controversiae* in the perspective of the political value of declamation. For the moment, I want simply to observe that the school themes allude not only to episodes of the Greco-Roman historiographical tradition, but also to individual figures. Latin literature's taste for *exempla* (inherited from aristocratic Roman culture generally) pervades even the practices of rhetoricians.[29] Marc van der Poel has catalogued all the *exempla* present in Latin declamation in a contribution that provides a convenient naming scheme.[30] From this study, we easily recognize the recurrence of names familiar to the annalistic tradition, almost always evoked in the most predictable terms: Manlius Torquatus (but also Lucius Brutus) for his severity with his son; Coruncanius or Cincinnatus for their virtuous poverty; the Scipios and Pompey the Great for their military victories; Gaius Marius or Crassus or Cicero as examples of the mutability of fortune; Cornelia as the exemplary mother; Lucretia or Virginia as models of female chastity; and so on. More interestingly, the perspective is almost always that of mainstream historiography and of a

---

28 See Lentano (2016b), 377 and n. 8.
29 See Berti (2007), 198–202.
30 Cf. van der Poel (2009).

conservative stripe. Thus, the Gracchi are sowers of discord and underminers of the Republic (*Minor* 268.19); Rutilius Rufus, persecuted by the Marians, represents an example of a virtuous man unjustly exiled (*Minor* 300.9); and Sulla, unpopular even with his own political party, is a model of cruelty (Seneca, *Controversiae* 2.4.4 and 9.2.19).

Beyond the reference to precise historical events or figures, what counts is the vision of history that Latin declamation engenders—a vision that is similar in important aspects to that of historiography in a strict sense. I am referring, in particular, to its tendency to perceive the present in terms of decadence in respect to a past that normally functions as an exemplar. The trope of *convicium saeculi* works in this way, lamenting the crisis of customs and loss of values—reduced to a stale *topos* but still capable of sinking its roots in a vision of history well established in Roman culture. In some cases, the lament has a more punctual consistency. Thus, in Seneca the Elder's *Controversia* 2.1, the rise of the civil wars is linked directly to the growth of wealth and reference to Rome's recent past is explicit: "When we were poor, we knew more tranquil times; we have waged civil wars when we covered the Capitoline in gold."[31] Seneca shares the image of the *aurea Capitolia* as a beloved or abhorred symbol of modernity with all of Augustan poetry, from Virgil to Propertius to Ovid. Similarly in *Minor* 349, about a father accused of dementia by his own *raptor* son for not pardoning him during the thirty days permitted by law, which would save him from capital punishment:

> If you had come into the hands of the one who cut off his son's head, who also covered himself with glory, or of he for whom the opinions of relatives and friends were sufficient, you would have had, I am sure, the time to complain. You would have had the time, I don't say to drag your father to court, but finally to address a request for clemency to him again.[32]

The text alludes to the well-known episode of Titus Manlius Torquatus, who in 340 BCE had his son (of the same name) beaten to death. The young Titus had been victorious in a duel, but had fought against the orders of his father as consul.[33] It also alludes to another severe father of the archaic period, who in 485 BCE put his son Spurius Cassius to death for aspiring to tyranny, after having

---

31 2.1.1: Quietiora tempora pauperes habuimus; bella civilia aurato Capitolio gessimus.
32 349.8: Tu, si incidisses in illum qui laudatas filii sui cervices amputavit, si incidisses in illum qui iudiciis propinquorum atque amicorum contentus fuit, opinor habuisses tempus querendi, habuisses tempus non dico deferendi patrem sed diutius rogandi.
33 Named mistakenly Lucius Manlius Torquatus in Shackleton Bailey (2006), vol. 1, 300–301, n. 8.

taken—according to the regular practice—the opinion of an informal counsel of friends and family. The conclusion of the long tirade is as follows:

> They were truly courageous men, they were heroes! They remembered that they sired children for the benefit of the Republic and believed it worthwhile to sacrifice them if this could serve as an example.[34]

Not by chance, in the immediately preceding text, this father had called those remote times *feliciora saecula*, just as the declaimer of Seneca's *Controversia* 2.1 speaks of *quietiora tempora*, blessed epochs "in which virtue was more widespread than it is today".[35]

Passages like this are found in historians such as Sallust and Livy. Livy includes a passage in which, referring to father–son relationships, he laments the crisis of paternal *auctoritas* in his own times, compared with the era of the Second Punic War, and refers precisely to a Manlius Torquatus.[36] Moreover, the *maiores* appear in declamations as the bearers of superior wisdom, especially in the field of legislation, which for obvious reasons is privileged in the context of declamation. Such passages are numerous, and Michael Winterbottom deserves credit for highlighting them. This is the case especially in some passages of *Minor* 252, where *actio inscripti maleficii* comes into play—that is, the act of "unwritten wrongdoing", a typical declamatory invention and lacking any correspondence in real law. Debate on the value of this specific procedure offers the occasion to celebrate the prudence of the ancestors:

> If these accusations fall under a specific law that ordains them, accuse me on this basis. But if this is not so, why do you raise a procedural exception under the scrupulousness of the ancestors and their refined intellects that put the law into writing?[37]

And again:

> It seems to me that our ancestors conceived this law with utmost care. Knowing that no wisdom is sufficiently great and no forecasting capability

---

34 349.8: Illi vere fortes et viri fuerunt qui cum hoc meminissent, liberos a se rei publicae gratia procreatos, bene inpendi crediderunt exemplo.
35 349.7: Si incidisses in illos felicioribus saeculis natos, cum quibus virtus magis commune bonum erat, non expectassent legem, non expectassent tricesimum diem.
36 26.22.15: Centuriam vero iuniorum seniores consulere voluisse quibus imperium suffragio mandaret, vix ut veri simile sit parentium quoque hoc saeculo vilis levisque apud liberos auctoritas fecit.
37 252.7: Haec crimina si quam aliam legem habent, transfer sane actionem meam; si nullam aliam habent, cur praescribis adversus maiorum diligentiam et exquisita ingenia quae <ius> scripserunt?

so certain as to imagine all the crimes that can be thought up by the mind of miscreants and to guard against these, with this law they wanted to place around all wickedness almost a kind of net, so to speak, so that whatever fault escaped the remedies provided by other laws could nevertheless by circumscribed.[38]

Even more interesting is the passage—uttered ironically—in *Minor* 264, because it deals with the only case of explicit reference to a Roman law, the *lex Voconia*, so that the appreciation of its elaboration is understood as so much recognition of the "indigenous" legal tradition:

Now men who are expert in legal processes are here to bring us to an understanding of the law. They want us to believe that the intention of the legislator is not what appears in the letter of the law. I, judges, remain however astonished by their cleverness. They are so superior to our ancestors, those founders of the law, those who through the laws and rights gave shape to a still rough popular, as to want us to believe that men so lacked the ability to express themselves clearly or that they lacked intelligence.[39]

The motif occurs elsewhere in nearly identical terms, for example in *Minor* 279.7 ("does it seem to you that our ancestors, those founders of the law, were less scrupulous, who brought those as yet disunited peoples to a sure form of life?") and in 350.5, where the *summa prudentia maiorum* is mentioned.[40] Here declamation comes close to the famous passage of Cicero, where the orator's persuasive speech and the constraint of law is merited with having brought men out of a state of nature and with having established them in politically organized communities; and to an equally well-known Ciceronian text, where the superior *sapientia* and *prudentia* of the *maiores* in the legislative field (the same words

---

38 252.8: Diligentissime maiores hanc videntur excogitasse legem, quod, cum scirent nullam tantam esse prudentiam, nullam immo tam certam divinationem ut omnia quaecumque ingeniis malorum excogitari umquam potuissent providentia caventium videret, hac lege omnem malitiam veluti quadam indagine cinxerunt, ut quidque aliarum legum effugisset auxilium quasi extrinsecus circumdaretur.

39 264.7: Nunc peritissimi litium homines ad interpretationem nos iuris adducunt. Non enim hanc esse legis voluntatem quae verbis ostendatur videri volunt. Quorum ego prudentiam, iudices, magnopere miror: tantum vicerunt illos maiores nostros, illos constitutores iuris, illos qui rudem civitatem legibus ac iure formarunt, ut hoc adprobare conentur, defuisse his sermonem, defuisse consilium.

40 279.7: An vero parum sancti illi videntur fuisse maiores, illi constitutores iuris, qui civitates adhuc velut antiquo illo errore confusas ad certam vivendi formam redegerunt? Seneca the Elder had already spoken of *prudentia* of the *maiores* (*Controversiae*, 4.7); other passages indicated by Winterbottom (1984) include *Declamationes minores* 308.3, 311.10, 320.3, and 370.1.

Culture in declamation

used by Pseudo-Quintilian) stand out for having established a punishment for patricide, which had been omitted from the laws of Solon on the naïve assumption that such a crime was impossible:[41]

> Our ancestors were much more careful. They understood that there is nothing so sacred that wickedness will not, at some time or another, attempt to violate—and for this reason they conceived a punishment for patricide very different from other punishments.[42]

Both in Pseudo-Quintilian and in Cicero, the *maiores* appear to be endowed with a superior capacity of foresight, thanks to which they are able to conceive of situations that others, less sensible than they, have not taken into account. The *maiores* are, moreover, always attributed extraordinary juridical creativity, as the occurrence in both authors of the verb *excogitare* suggests. In one case, they have conceived of a punishment that is entirely unique: the penalty of the sack, which in its cruelty mirrored the extreme nature of the crime it sanctioned—patricide. In the other case, the creativity consists in formulating a law that in its wording seems deliberately fashioned to not leave out any crime that might escape legislators' awareness and thus lack provisions in existing law. The declaimer's words are uttered in the imaginary context of Sophistopolis, and yet they reflect conditioned reflexes of Roman culture: in this case, the belief that they possessed a legal system superior to any other thanks to the wisdom of the *maiores*.

All these aspects do not amount to a comprehensive philosophy of history. However, they reflect a widespread sentiment in Roman culture. This has an interesting consequence: in passages such as those we have cited, the profile of the imaginary City of the Rhetoricians ends up coinciding with Rome itself. The past to which the protagonists of the declamations refer is one familiar to their readers from the *exempla* of virtues and of vices constantly evoked in the Latin historiographical tradition; those *maiores* of whom the rhetoricians speak are the same as those to which Cicero and Livy allude. The line between the fictitious world of the declaimers and the real world of the city shrinks almost to disappearing. At the same time, the contents of different declamations confirm the pessimistic vision of history of which they are themselves bearers. Populated by often unspeakable passions, grubby claims on power, petty hereditary aspirations, thirst for sex and money, the *controversiae* paint a picture

---

41 In general, cf. Cicero, *De oratore*, 1.197, where the *prudentia* of *nostri maiores* is juxtaposed to the laws of Solon, Lycurgus, and Draco.
42 *Pro Sexto Roscio*, 70: Quanto nostri maiores sapientius! Qui cum intellegerent nihil esse tam sanctum quod non aliquando violaret audacia, supplicium in parricidas singulare excogitaverunt.

of a degenerate world that has abandoned forever any aura of greatness and looks back, nostalgically, to the *feliciora saecula* behind it—aware that those times are lost and never to return.

Let us come, finally, to the most expansive dossier: that of the relation between declamation and vast narrative and literary imaginary of the ancient world. Here, too, there is a micro- and a macro-level. On the plane of specific motifs, it is not difficult to trace declamation's literary ancestries—for example, in the description of storm scenes (as in Seneca's 7.1), a *topos* of Latin literature from the archaic period, or in the theme of *odia fraterna* studied by Emanuele Berti and exemplified by the controversy that opens Seneca's anthology.[43] What is more, declamations have been called "novels in miniature", with themes such as that of the daughter of the pirate (given in Chapter 1 and discussed again later). More generally, one thread of research, promoted by Danielle van Mal-Maeder and followed by Lucia Pasetti and Nicola Hömke, has always insisted on the fictional character of declamation: above all, the complete pieces that can be read in the larger collection of Pseudo-Quintilian often exhibit a strongly literary character, expressed through frequent allusions to tragedy, in the quest for suspense, in the spectacularization of situations. In this sense, declamation configured itself as an excellent example of consumption literature, capable of satisfying the Roman public's hunger for entertainment.

This approach has the merit of underscoring the literary components of declamation: its character as a sophisticated intellectual game, liable to be undertaken in forms disconnected from precise didactic contexts; its connection with narrative and in particular with the novel. I would not, however, agree in making a rigid distinction between school declamations and "show" declamations (*Schaudeklamationen*), as Hömke proposes.[44] In the hands of the most promising and skilled students or the most talented teachers, and on occasion of the "open days" when schools were open to the larger public, it is clear that performances reached a level of literariness that probably was not expected of the everyday practice in the classroom, without it being possible to delineate typological differences too precisely.

Research has also led to the understanding that the relationship between school rhetoric and literature is bidirectional. Controversies influence other literary genres, as long acknowledged, sometimes critically for the excessive "rhetoricization" that such influence brought about. Often the influence goes in the other direction, however. To give only a couple of examples, highlighted

---

43 Berti (2007), 311ff. On both themes see also Bernstein (2013a).
44 Hömke (2007).

Culture in declamation

again by Danielle van Mal-Maeder: the theme of cannibalism developed in *Cadaveribus pasti*, Pseudo-Quintilian's declamation that deals with the dramatic case of a city devastated by famine, whose surviving inhabitants are compelled to eat human bodies, alludes to the myth of Thyestes in terms similar to those of Seneca's tragedy.[45] The final peroration, with the picture it paints of the infernal punishments that await those who have eaten human flesh, has resemblances to Seneca's *Phaedra*, as well. The eighth *Maior*, *Gemini languentes*, also appears to allude to this *pièce*; there, a mother promises to the twin dead after vivisection to collect and recompose his limbs—evoking Theseus looking upon the body of Hippolytus in the finale of Seneca's tragedy.[46] Through these allusions, declamation emphasizes its literary chops. In the latter case, we note, too, a taste for scenes of dismemberment and mutilation that characterizes much of Latin poetry of the early imperial period. Giovanna Longo (2008) has also highlighted numerous literary reminiscences in the twinned declamations on *Odii potio* (14 and 15), of Pseudo-Quintilian's major collection, where a young man makes an accusation of poisoning against the *meretrix* from whom he has received a drink that causes him to be rejected.[47] Lexical as well as more substantive allusions to Catullus's poetry—and more generally to elegy—and to situations of comedy demonstrate the vast literary background declaimers were able to exploit and filter in their compositions.

It is not possible to trace every connection between declamation and narrative here. Moreover, such connections occur at different levels, including cases where novels feature scenes that recall the settings of *controversiae*, with two parties required to state their claims before an audience.[48] Let us consider a highly instructive example, then. Seneca's *Controversia* 1.2, whose theme we translated in Chapter 1, presents an intricate case: a virgin has been abducted by pirates and sold to a pimp, who compels her to prostitute herself. The woman succeeds, however, in convincing her clients to pay her without actually sleeping with her. When a soldier refuses to go along with this request, she kills him. She is then brought to court, absolved, and restored to her family; later, she tries to enter a priestly order that is easily identifiable as the Vestals, familiar to the Roman audience. As always, the theme of the *controversia* is accompanied by a law,

---

45 See van Mal-Maeder (2007), 16. On this declamation (and its relationship with epic, tragedy and novel) cf. Stramaglia (2003); Bernstein (2013a), 104–108; Cappello (2016); Nocchi (2017); Hömke (2021); Ravallese (2021).
46 See van Mal-Maeder (2007), 80–81. On this declamation cf. Stramaglia (1999); Bernstein (2013b), 64–74.
47 Cf. Longo (2008). See also Calboli (2010a).
48 E.g., Apuleius, *Metamorphoses*, 3.2-10. See van Mal-Maeder (2007), 125–127.

which imposes on the aspiring priestess the requirement of being "chaste and the daughter of chaste parents, pure and the daughter of pure parents". The debate thus revolves around a question of *status finitivus* and more precisely a *duplex quaestio finitiva*, because definitions need to be given both for "chaste" (and "pure") and "daughter of chaste parents" (or "of pure parents").[49]

An interesting discussion of the categories of *castitas* and *puritas* in Roman culture follows. But this does not interest us so much as the improbable misfortunes the rhetoricians envisage for their "harlot priestess" (as in the title of the *controversia*), for making the case more complicated and for putting the talent of the students to the test. If abduction by pirates is a common motif of various literary genres, beginning with comedy, the bordello episode has a specific parallel in the Greek novel *Anthia and Habrocomes* by Xenophon of Ephesus, likely belonging to the late first/second century CE. The protagonists of this story are also abducted by pirates and separated after marriage. Naturally, Anthia is very beautiful, as heroines of novels always are, and all who encounter her fall in love—to the point that she, too, is forced to pick up a sword and kill one of her suitors when he refuses to be persuaded and tries to take her by force (4.5). The situation of the *controversia* is also closely matched by Anthia's sale to a pimp of Tarentum, after she arrives in Italy. To preserve her chastity, the protagonist of the novel fakes an epileptic fit, thanks to which she escapes the visitors of the bordello who have already gathered in large numbers and who are ready to pay a handsome fee to sleep with her (5.7). The story of Tarsia is also similar to that of the harlot priestess. Tarsia is the protagonist of the late antique novel *History of Apollonius, King of Tyre*. She is abducted by pirates, sold to a pimp of Mitylene, and also persuades her clients with the story of her misadventures.[50] We recognize that even in cases like this it is not possible, and perhaps not even important, to determine the exact relationship between the novel and declamation. If, in the past, an evolutionary account has prevailed—viewing the rhetorical "novel in miniature" as the matrix of novelistic developments—today it seems more reasonable to suppose that rhetorical teachers and narrators drew on the same shared imaginary, in which motifs circulated widely and were adopted into very different literary genres.

Another aspect of the relationship between school rhetoric and literature involves tragedy and therefore myth, which is the principal resource of the tragic theatre.[51] The presence of myth in the rhetorical *controversiae* manifests itself

---

49 Cf. Lentano (2017b).
50 Cf. Morales (2005), 218–220.
51 On the long-studied relationship between Seneca's tragedy and declamation cf. recently Casamento (2015b); Paré-Rey (2015).

mostly indirectly—not, that is, through explicit allusions to this or that figure of the mythological universe, but more subtly through the use of narrative elements that the reader is called upon to recognize despite their re-adaptation within the new framework where they are found. Thus, Danielle van Mal-Maeder and Graziana Brescia have drawn attention to Pseudo-Quintilian's *Minor* 299, *Ossa eruta parricidae*, whose female protagonist, torn between the law of the city that forbids violating tombs and her father's deathbed command to disinter his son—guilty of his murder—recalls the figure of Antigone:

> *Patricides should be expelled without burial. Legal action is allowed for violation of a tomb.* On his deathbed, a father entrusts his daughter with avenging him, stating that he has been poisoned by his two sons. The girl presents the charge against them. Pending trial, one of the two kills himself and is buried in the family cemetery. After the other is condemned and has been expelled without burial, the girl disinters the bones of the one who has been buried and casts them out. She is accused of violating his tomb.[52]

Another case of mythic reuse is Seneca the Elder's *Controversia* 1.6.[53] Here, a son is captured by pirates and kept prisoner in expectation of a ransom. As the young man awaits the intervention of his father, the daughter of the pirate captain falls in love with him, and promises to free him if he agrees to marry her and take her away. The plan is quickly realized and the two return together to the protagonist's city of origin. But an *orba* appears—the rich heiress who is the Roman equivalent of the Greek *epíkleros*—and the father forces his son to abandon his young bride (the lawfulness of the marriage is in any case doubtful) and to take the new woman as his wife. When the son refuses, he is disinherited. In this narrative design, it is not difficult to detect the myth of Medea and Jason, also marked by marriage request, the flight of the two lovers from Colchis to Greece, and finally the crisis between the hero and the "barbarian" witch when the possibility arises of a more advantageous and more honourable match, with the daughter of the king of Corinth.

But declamation draws on myth in a selective way, taking on only some of its traits, and the borrowing only goes so far as to allow the school theme to channel it along well-worn paths: in this case, the conflict between obedience to

---

52 PARRICIDAE INSEPULTI ABICIANTUR. SEPULCRI VIOLATI SIT ACTIO. Decedens pater mandavit filiae ultionem, dicens se duorum filiorum veneno perire. Puella reos postulavit. Inter moras unus se occidit et sepultus est in monumentis maiorum. Alterum cum damnasset et insepultum proiecisset, eius quoque qui sepultus fuerat ossa eruit et abiecit. Accusatur violati sepulcri. Cf. van Mal-Maeder (2003); Brescia (2015b); for the law, Krapinger (2016).

53 See Lentano (2010).

a father (who, moreover, had not ransomed the young man quickly) and sincere attachment to the woman to whom he owes his safety, a conflict ending up in the most classic *abdicatio*.

The influence of the Theban myth, and of the particular reading that Euripides's *Phoenician Women* gives to it, can easily be recognized in a theme such as that of *Minor* 326:

> Tormented by plague, they send an ambassador to consult the oracle. The oracle responds that they need to sacrifice the ambassador's son. Returning to the city, the ambassador reports that rituals were required, while to his son he confesses the truth. The rituals are undertaken, but the plague does not end. Then the son puts himself forward in the assembly and killed himself. The pestilence ends, and the ambassador is accused of harming the State.[54]

In the tragedy, the Athenian playwright introduces the figure of Menoeceus, who, it appears, was unknown to preceding variants of the myth. When Eteocles asks Creon to consult the seer Tiresias, to learn how to defeat the Argive army besieging the city, he reveals that Theban victory depends on sacrificing Creon's son—Menoeceus precisely, who must be sacrificed to Ares (834ff.). Following the departure of Tiresias, Creon tries everything to persuade Menoeceus to flee before the oracle's reply is known. The young man pretends to agree to his father's request, and then, alone, reveals to the Chorus through a monologue his real intent to take his own life to ensure the victory of the city that produced him. As may be seen, despite the different context—war in one case, plague in the other—tragedy and declamation present close analogies, especially in the father's attempt to save his son's life and in the son's choice to hasten the sacrifice for the common good.

In other cases, there is no specific myth in the background, but a kind of mytheme or motif that recurs across a series of related stories. Thus, Seneca's *Controversia* 7.1 presents the case of a son who, condemned in a domestic trial for patricide and put to sea by his brother on a decommissioned boat, encounters some pirates as he drifts at sea and becomes their leader. As their captain, he captures his father, whom he releases without ransom. The theme concludes with the father's return and disinheritance of the brother, evidently for having failed to fully carry out the job of avenging the presumed patricide.[55] This recalls the

---

54 Qui pestilentia laborabant miserunt legatum ad oraculum petendum. Responsum est ei filium ipsius immolandum esse. Ille nuntiavit civitati sacra desiderari; filio verum confessus est. Sacris finitis pestilentia non est finita. Filius processit in contionem et se ipse interfecit. Finita pestilentia reus est legatus laesae rei publicae.

55 Cf. Lentano (2012).

motif—typical of the mythic biographies of founders—of the abandoned baby who not only survives, but also overcomes the status of outcast and becomes the advocate of a new state of things (the foundation of a city, the introduction of new techniques, or something else)—a motif attested widely across different cultures, whether in the myth of the Akkadian king Sargon, the story of Moses or of the twins Romulus and Remus, or some variants of the myth of Oedipus.[56]

As seems obvious even from the brief account given here, when school rhetoric absorbs episodes and motifs of myth into its universe, it subjects them to a process of degradation. The hero Jason and the princess Medea, daughter of the king of Colchis, become a generic *adulescens* and the daughter of a pirate captain—certainly also "barbarian", yet not coming from a fabulous kingdom in the East, but from a radically "other" world like that of the pirates is in declamation. As for that other princess of myth, the beautiful Glauke, she is substituted by an anonymous *orba* whose only claim on the young man is the wealth she brings as a dowry. Similarly, the vicissitudes that bring Sargon, Moses, and Romulus to be leaders of their respective peoples are reduced in *controversia* to the much less honourable rise of the son, suspected of patricide, to the helm of a pirate fleet he encountered by chance. Declamation constructs a world rich in twists and turns and reversals of fortune, but still decidedly workaday and banal, deprived of that allure of greatness that is required of the sublime in myth. Myth is thus programmatically "unheroized" and reduced to an often dark reality, in which characters are motivated by murky reasoning and petty passions—similar in some sense to what has happened to the heroic age in certain rewritings of the Trojan myth (Dio of Prusa, Dictys of Crete, Dares the Phrygian, all basically contemporaneous with the period of the declamatory collections): it has become a hapless land devoid of heroes.

Sometimes, however, declamations do reach heights of sublimity. I have already mentioned Seneca the Elder's *Controversia* 1.2, about the woman who, after being abducted by pirates and sold to a pimp, claims virginity when applying for the role of Vestal. I have also underscored certain affinities with Greek novels of the imperial period. We can add that the motif of the "virgin harlot" returns in late antique narrative and even in hagiography, with all those saints from Agnes to Thecla who are forced by their pagan torturers to prostitute themselves as retaliation for not having disavowed their faith and yielded to their sexual requests. As Stelios Panayotakis has documented, this theme reaches even Shakespeare's *Pericles, Prince of Tyre*.[57] For the rhetoricians who devised

---

56 For another example of a motif taken from myth cf. Lentano (2018b); see also Rolle (2018); Larosa (2020); Brescia (2021).
57 Cf. Panayotakis (2002).

that theme, however, the most immediate referent must have been Greek and Latin New Comedy, where women beloved by young men are often courtesans serving a pimp. In comedy, the enamoured young man is often compelled to break off the relationship and marry a "respectable" woman, as happens to Pamphilus in Terence's *Hecyra*. It also happens that the young man is able to prove the *meretrix*'s free and honourable birth, thus making her a legitimate matrimonial option. However, when this occurs, it is necessary to show that even as a prostitute the woman *only* slept with her future husband—to preserve a fundamental anthropological compatibility.

In the Senecan *controversia*, however, the female protagonist does not aspire to marriage, but to a priesthood. She is not then called upon to show her own link with a single partner, but the absence of any stain on her physical integrity, despite her prolonged sojourn with pirates and then in the service of a pimp. The debate anthologized by Seneca thus ends up touching on questions of a high moral character. At least in the interventions that reject easy and distasteful vulgarity, *Controversia* 1.2 comes across as a reflection on key notions of Roman religious thought, such as chastity and purity—the only one the Roman world has left us, at least before the advent of Christianity.

However partial and cursory this survey might be, declamation nevertheless stands out as a decidedly composite genre, capable of drawing on many cultural experiences and many texts—literary in a strict sense, philosophical, historiographic. Still to explore are declamation's close ties with juridical reflection; this we will do in Chapter 6. Unravelling declamation's complex network of allusions and influences is not a straightforward operation; it must be done text by text, in order to clarify the richness of the hints and models that the rhetoricians kept present and put to use. In any case, recent studies put the lie to the idea that these are creations aimed at the simple exhibition of linguistic flourishes and rhetorical virtuosity. Instead, each declamation appears as the precipitate of a vast and multiform culture, belonging to a society that has behind it centuries of textual accumulation and can draw on this deep reservoir to recombine elements in a virtually infinite number of variations.

5

THE POLITICS OF DECLAMATION

The meticulous prosopographical study of Seneca the Elder published some years ago by Elvira Migliario concludes that the anthology preserves materials that date to around 35 BCE, extending to cover the entire period of Tiberius.[1] Thus, the moment when school declamation reaches its fullest maturity coincides with the upheaval of the last civil war, with the rise of Octavian (later Augustus) to the heights of the Republican regime, and the slow transformation of this regime into a government of one, with the definitive consolidation of the new political situation linked to the succession of Tiberius, when it was clear that the very long reign of Augustus was not a parenthesis in the institution history of Rome but a turning point without real alternatives and irreversible. It would be reasonable to expect that this turn of events—which appear decisive to us, and which were perceived as such by those living through them—were echoed also in the environment of the rhetorical schools. And yet looking at Seneca's anthology, so rich in stories and populated by more than 100 orators and rhetoricians, does not seem to show any trace of this politics. To tell the truth, there have been those who have seen in the schools of declamation a sort of lair of nostalgic philo-Republicans, almost the expression of an intellectual resistance to the new political reality. And in some cases, the profile that Seneca provides of this or that declaimer does reveal nostalgic attitudes. For example, Seneca marvels that in the prime of the Augustan principate and thus "in such an absolute situation of peace", Titus Labienus still nursed his "Pompeian spirits".[2] But this attitude characterizes a very small set among the many mentioned by Seneca, and, except for very rare cases, does not influence their "professional" activity. So the idea of the schools as sites of protest against the imperial regime should probably be abandoned.

Naturally, the question of Seneca's own political position—he is often considered a nostalgic lover of the past—is different, and not strictly relevant to our discussion; so I will limit myself to only a brief consideration. In fact, the

1 Migliario (2007), 21.
2 *Controversiae*, 10, *praef.* 5.

figure of Augustus is treated with great respect in Seneca's *Orators and Rhetoricians*, and the forbearance the *princeps* showed towards disrespectful expressions of dissent is often praised there.[3] However, there is one aspect Seneca expressly condemns, even if this condemnation is attenuated by a certain caution: the repression of intellectual nonconformity—a question that, evidently, as a scholar and above all as the author of a historical work that touched on hot contemporary topics, Seneca must have had great interest in. Certainly, the long passage in which he recounts how the historical work of Labienus was burned in Augustus's final years—precisely, one supposes, because of the "Pompeian spirits" that motivated its author and probably informed his writings—is the harshest and most politically engaged of the entire Senecan corpus.[4] At that point, however, Seneca took for granted what must have been the official version of the episode, according to which the Senate ordered the destruction of the book scrolls on the initiative of unnamed "personal enemies" of the historian. Naturally, Seneca was too savvy not to realize that the Senate would not have acted without the emperor's approval, but prudently chose to follow the "vulgate" the emperor intended to circulate about the disagreeable event. Seneca explains that this "novel punishment" of burning was conceived against dissident literature "then *for the first time*" (emphasis added): he knew very well that there had been at least one other episode, in 25 CE, when the work of Cremutius Cordus was consigned to the flames, for similar reasons. Seneca may even have been an eyewitness of the latter episode, but he omits any mention of it, except to take the satisfaction of quoting in laudatory terms two fragments of Cremutius, whose work, like Labienus's, had returned into circulation as a kind of posthumous compensation for the regime's treatment (*Suasoriae* 6, 19 and 23).

Though of great interest, this is outside the scope of our study. But it is worth asking if the impression of declamation's absolute "apoliticalness" stands up to deeper examination of the collections in our possession. In the first place, we know from Seneca again—who is the only one to provides first-hand information in this regard—that prominent members of the political class participated in the practice of declamation as a form of refined intellectual *divertissement*. Asinius Pollio is one example. But Augustus himself also occasionally joined in sessions of the rhetorical schools, accompanied by his entourage (Agrippa, Maecenas).[5] This may have been part of the patronage of intellectual activity in general that the *princeps* tried to exercise, and reveals his interest in monitoring

---

3   See the discussion in Torri (2002–03) and now Lentano (2019).
4   *Controversiae*, 10, *praef.* 5–8; cf. Canfora (2015), 167–168.
5   As in the case recorded in *Controversiae*, 2.4.12–13; cf. Berti (2007), 38 and n. 1; Rizzelli (2012), 293–295.

from up close a branch of the educational system that was beginning to take on more and more relevance within the schooling of the future ruling class, and in particular of that sector of society which Augustan politics was aimed at nourishing. Elsewhere, Seneca reports judgments expressed by the *princeps* regarding individual declaimers (Lucius Vinicius in 2.5.20; Quintus Haterius in 4, *praef.* 7) or, vice versa, expressions used by a declaimer that relate to the emperor (Varius Geminus in 6.8.2; Crantor in 10.5.12)—even if we cannot know if such utterances came in the context of sessions attended by Augustus or on some other occasion. Unfortunately, we do not possess much similar information for later periods, but a couple of exceptions help illuminate the development of relations between political power and the activity of the schools.

From two passages of Severan historian Dio Cassius we learn that Caligula exiled several teachers of rhetoric accused of having "declaimed against the tyrants" and that Domitian even executed some (respectively 59.20.6 and 67.12.5: the figures in question are Secundus Carrinas and the "sophist Maternus", as Dio calls him). Unfortunately, this information is not embellished with further details about the figures in question and the reasons for their conflict with the two emperors. However, I am less certain now of what I have claimed in the past that reference to the professional activity of these two rhetoricians was only a cover for other, more substantial political motivations as a basis for punitive measures. Especially in the case of Domitian, it is well known that he was inclined to see malicious allusions everywhere, and often reacted to these outrageously—for example, when he not only destroyed the historical work of a certain Hermogenes of Tarsus (the content of which we do not know) but also punished the scribes who had copied it, lest the content of that text survive at all (Suetonius, *Life of Domitian*, 10.1). It is possible, then, that some emperors saw in the activities of some schoolmasters signs of protest against their regimes—the more dangerous they appeared to be, the more hidden they were behind the commonest themes of rhetorical exercise, as sources external to the world of the schools seem to confirm (e.g., Juvenal 7.150–54). The tyrants of tragedy as well as those of declamation nourished such interpretations, moreover. Under Tiberius, Mamercus Aemilius Scaurus, a political and literary figure, as well as an adherent of the schools of declamation mentioned by Seneca the Elder, was punished because the emperor had read his tragedy *Atreus* as an allusion to his ferocity (among others, again Dio Cassius is our source: 58.24.3–4). Several decades later, one of the protagonists of Tacitus's *Dialogus de oratoribus*, Curiatius Maternus, states that he conceived the plot of another tragedy about the same myth, *Thyestes*, containing unequivocal references to contemporary political reality, after one of his earlier works, on the figure of Cato Uticensis, provoked discontent and resentment within the imperial court, presumably for its philo-Republicanism (2–3). We cannot rule out that Tacitus's Curiatius may be related to the "sophist Maternus" executed by Domitian for anti-tyrannical sentiments.[6] Both tragedy and school exercises could serve, then, as an easy alibi for alluding to real "tyrants" in power in Rome, or at least exposed themselves to the risk of being read in this way and of being censored. The fortune of the myth of Atreus and Thyestes throughout the Julio-Claudian period, including allusions to that myth in declamation, is probably also explainable in this way.

This helps us understand the problem of the "politicalness" of the declamations concerning tyrants and tyrannicide: to what degree they might allude to the principate, or could be read as such. Scholars are hardly unanimous on this score. Whereas Emanuele Berti considers quite unreasonable "many scholars' attempt to relate the tyrants of the *controversiae* to the concrete figure of the *princeps* and the contemporaneous debate around the form of the principate", for Laurent Pernot, "We should ... consider the possibility that declamations concerning tyrants have had implications in the contemporaneous reality of the declaimers".[7] On a question like this, it is difficult to draw firm conclusions, and we probably need to trust the interpretation that appears most likely. Personally, I am inclined to attribute to school themes about tyranny a very strong degree of allusiveness to present realities of imperial power—not because they refer to this or that emperor (which would have been difficult given the strongly stereotyped character of such themes), but because they offer an opportunity to reflect on the nature and limits of this very power, reflection that in all likelihood seemed pressing given the new historical-political context in which the declaimers operated.

Reflection on questions of power and its legitimate scope cuts through declamation in its entirety: the power of a father to disinherit a disobedient son; the power of a husband to divorce his wife; the power for prize-winners to violate other laws because of the total freedom given to them in choosing a prize, and so on. In all these cases, and in many others, what is at stake is determining what an individual can and cannot do, based on the prerogatives he or she can claim. The debates that every *controversia* stages—where the actions of each party are accurately weighed up, to establish if they have gone beyond the bounds in trying to take advantage of these prerogatives—are nothing but an endless series of reflections on forms of power and its legitimate exercise, an intrinsically political theme if ever there was one. If all this is true, then *controversiae* that

---

6 Some have even suggested they are the same person; see Vössing (2010), esp. 311–312.
7 Cf. respectively Berti (2007), 100, n. 2 and Pernot (2007), 217–218; similarly, Schwartz (2016), 267.

have tyrants as protagonists can also be interpreted as a reflection on this special form of authority, but with a specific and decisive difference.

In all the cases we have mentioned, the prerogatives of the parties are established by law. A father can disinherit a son or a husband divorce his wife because in Sophistopolis there are laws that give them this right. And it is a (fictional, but that is irrelevant) law that awards a prize to a *vir fortis* or to a tyrannicide. Conflict arises in such cases either because the counterparty has the right of appeal—that is, the chance to oppose an *abdicatio* or disinheritance in court when it is deemed unjust—or because, in the case of *controversiae* about prizes, the hero's request conflicts with other principles protected by law, as when the *vir fortis* chooses to wed a Vestal Virgin or his own daughter. This problem does not exist with respect to the tyrant, of course. The power of the autocrat is by definition unconstrained and can be exercised against any existing law, and despite anything belonging to the sphere of law or the less formalized but equally binding sphere of *mores*.

This feature of tyrannical power is not unlike the authority of Roman emperors, particularly as we get farther and farther from Augustus and into the Julio-Claudian period, until, in the Severan period, it is formalized by Ulpian in the famous adage *quod principi placuit legis habet vigorem* (*Digesta*, 1.4.1 pr.). So the tyrants of declamation are a sort of permanent warning against the risks of unconstrained power that has no limits on its absolute will. If, as has been claimed, certain despotic figures of Senecan drama—above all Atreus—are a kind of contrafactual *paideía* addressed to Nero (complementary to the lesson given to the same emperor in *De clementia*), the image of the abyss of violence into which unconstrained power risks falling, then similar reasoning can be applied to the school controversies, which teach each new generation of the élite how tyranny is incompatible with the life of a city governed by laws and how in the face of despotism the only possible response is tyrannicide. It is perhaps this lesson, implicit but no less clear, that nourished the suspicion of emperors like Caligula and Domitian.

Finally, there are cases in which the connection to political realities is even stronger. Ida Gilda Mastrorosa has emphasized an episode reported by Seneca the Elder (*Suasoria* 2.21), related to a *controversia* about "harm to the Republic", against a matron who refused the womanly duty of producing children.[8] Mastrorosa has shown that the episode, normally dated to the late Augustan period, should instead be attributed to the period when the *lex Iulia de maritandis ordinibus* was promulgated—around 18 BCE—to encourage the "civic duty" of productive marriage, with ramified awards and incentives. This law appears to

---

8   Mastrorosa (2008), 68–69.

have been echoed almost immediately in the schools and inspired the elaboration of themes problematizing its content and bringing under a critical lens this Augustan doctrine, all under the cover of harmless declamatory exercise. If Antonio Stramaglia—who reads an allusion to the legend of the birth of the future Augustus by the god Apollo in the theme of Seneca's *Suasoria* 4.4—is right, we would have a case in which the rhetoricians recuperate "in real time" a central aspect of the ideology of the principate.[9]

Now, up to this point, I have spoken only about *controversiae*, but a survey of the possible political meanings of declamation must also consider that other product of the rhetorical schools, *suasoriae*. Unfortunately, this is a body of texts that has reached us in very reduced form: only seven complete texts that Seneca the Elder appended to the ten books of *controversiae*. Recently, references to the Augustan age identifiable in the background of the preserved themes have been meticulously uncovered by Elvira Migliario.[10] Here, it will be sufficient to refer to the two *suasoriae* (the sixth and seventh) relating to the figure of Cicero and in particular to his murder by the triumvirate of which Augustus was a member:

Suasoria 6: Cicero deliberates whether to ask for mercy from Antony.[11]

Suasoria 7: Cicero deliberates whether to throw his own writings into the fire, following a promise of immunity from Antony if he should do so.[12]

The reading of these texts (and of Seneca's *Controversia* 7.2, on the same theme) shows, among other things, that the declaimers were collectively aligned with the regime's version of history, which imputed to Antony alone the guilt of that terrible murder. With very rare exceptions, the personal responsibility of Octavian—who chose to sacrifice his political mentor on the altar of an alliance with two ex-Caesarians—remains largely in the shadows: difficult to say whether because of explicit pressure by those in power or owing to spontaneous self-censoring by teachers themselves (or even by Seneca who selectively preserves their positions). As for the controversy on Popillius (the theme of which was given in Chapter 4), its theme almost fastidiously insists on the guilt of Antony as the sole instigator of Cicero's murder, but also poses a question of great political significance: to what extent is it possible to make a legal case out of the Civil War, putting on trial the actual perpetrators of crimes committed

---

9 Cf. Stramaglia (2016b).
10 Cf. Migliario (2007); on the first *suasoria*, La Bua (2015) is also interesting.
11 Deliberat Cicero, an Antonium deprecetur.
12 Deliberat Cicero, an scripta sua comburat promittente Antonio incolumitatem, si fecisset.

in the feverish climate of the triumvirate and that purport to be justified by that climate.

But sometimes *suasoriae* go further. In the second book of Seneca's *On Benefits*, the author affirms that "it is customarily discussed" whether Brutus acted appropriately when he took the life of Caesar, who surely had spared his.[13] The expression makes us think that Seneca, who was so entrenched in the environment of the rhetorical schools thanks to his father's teaching, is alluding to a *suasoria* theme, in which the future assassin of Caesar deliberated over the step he was about to take.[14] We can infer that, in the school context, the episode of Caesaricide was transformed into an exercise around the declamatory category of ingratitude—somewhat as in the aforementioned *controversia* 7.2 of Seneca the Elder, the murder of Cicero was seen as the outcome of Popillius's vicious nature, willing to kill the patron who had once successfully defended him on a capital charge. Indeed, Popillius was imagined to be brought to court *de moribus*, and not for the assassination as such. This might seem to be a prudent (if not actually obscurantist) strategy—a way to defang these episodes, by omitting their more politically embarrassing aspects and bringing them back within the boundaries of relations and of exquisitely "private" and personal faults. But that would be mistaken. The sources on Caesaricide show that the figure of Brutus was highly controversial *also* because of having benefited from Caesar, and thus of having been bound to him by in a relationship of gratitude, which the act of homicide fractured. Whatever the chosen perspective, the *suasoria* on which *On Benefits* draws seems to have thematized moral judgements of Caesar's murder—a meaningful choice, when we consider that the young Claudius, not yet emperor, abandoned the idea of composing an historical work covering the aftermath of the Ides of March, persuaded that it was not possible to speak freely of it; that in the era of Nero was still possible to be condemned for keeping an effigy of Cassius at home; and that even under the *optimus princeps* Trajan it was dangerous to demonstrate admiration for Brutus publicly.[15] So the declaimers—unlike Silius Italicus in epic—did not hide behind Rome's remote past, material that was less appealing but less dangerous, and sometimes took the risk of touching on the most charged episodes of recent history. We should not underestimate this courageous choice, which may have attracted to the schools the less-than-benevolent attention of suspicious emperors.

---

13 2.20.1: Disputari de M. Bruto solet, an debuerit accipere ab divo Iulio vitam, cum occidendum eum iudicaret.
14 Cf. Kohl (1915), 107, n. 427; Lentano (2009a); Stramaglia (2015), 157–158.
15 Cf. respectively Suetonius, *Divus Claudius*, 41.2; Tacitus, *Annales*, 16.7; Pliny the Younger, *Epistulae*, 1.173.

The fact is that the bloody period between the Ides of March (44 BCE) and the beginning of the triumvirate's proscriptions (around the end of 43 BCE) remained, for the entire Julio-Claudian era and to some degree even after, a sort of past that does not pass, to which historiography and literature constantly returned, recognizing in it the roots of the present and the cradle of the imperial regime. No surprise, then, that in the period of Seneca the figure of Brutus and his political act were a recurring subject of debate in the schools. We can assume that this debate was conducted cautiously, as in the case of Cicero's assassination, because the emperors were sensitive to how that crucial historical event was reconstructed and interpreted. Cremutius Cordus was brought to trial under Tiberius, in 25 CE, for having praised Brutus and called Cassius, Caesar's killer, the last of the Romans. Quintilian informs us that when Cordus's work returned to circulation under Caligula, it was expurgated "of the parts that have harmed their author", and therefore presumably of the admiring judgement of Cassius that was the cause of its censoring.[16]

Finally, the question of the "politics" of declamation can be addressed from another, perhaps more substantive point of view. In research of the last thirty years, scholars have often insisted on the presumed "conservative" character of school rhetoric. Declamations are thought to offer a rigorous education in the traditional values of the élite, teaching its young members exactly what their fathers would want to hear. In short, they have been seen as a powerful means of socializing new generations to the dominant values of society.[17] The *controversiae* are thought to deliver the core values of Romanness; confirm distinctions of status and of gender; reinforce traditional roles (especially that of the father); teach what it means to exist and to think as a Roman, and educate élite males to the governing role they will one day be called upon to exercise over their subordinates (whether these are children, wives, slaves, fellow citizens, or subjects). According to this broad vision, declamations are not "political" in the sense of endorsing a specific type of government, or (worse) recommending a republican alternative to the imperial regime, but by virtue of imagining the present as the direct descendant of the Roman values and roles of the past, to the preservation and transmission of which the rhetorical school definitively contribute.

This way of viewing declamatory rhetoric has become so entrenched in scholarship that it is often taken for granted and has the force of an *idée reçue*. We need

---

16 Quintilian 10.1.104: Habet amatores—nec immerito—Cremuti libertas, quamquam circumcisis quae dixisse ei nocuerat.
17 Cf,. e.g., Beard (1993); Imber (1997 and 2001); Kaster (2001); Bloomer (2007); Corbeill (2007); Hömke (2007); for an opposing view, see Friend (1999); recent discussion in Lendon (2022), 14–25, with further bibliography.

The politics of declamation

to ask, however, if this view accurately captures the state of affairs that emerges from a comprehensive reading of declamation as attested in surviving collections. To my lights, this view is only partially correct. Declamation does not actually question social hierarchies and established gender roles. In the school themes, children are subordinate to fathers and must obey; wives must be faithful to their husbands and must obey; women and minors have no right to speak in court and their interests must be represented at trial by a patron; freedmen and slaves are divided by an insurmountable chasm; and so on. Sophistopolis is an imaginary place, but what Umberto Eco once said about possible worlds holds for it too: unless explicitly stated otherwise, their functioning must be considered in line with that of the real world.[18]

But this is only part of the truth. Because the *controversiae* are, above all, an ongoing reflection on power and its limits, established hierarchies are constantly open to challenges and oppositions, to which declamation gives space and a voice, persuasively articulating their reasons and giving them an equal platform. It is true that fathers maintain the position of primacy that Roman culture always recognized for them. In this sense, to claim that declamation works to confirm *patria potestas* and contests only its excesses or abuses is obvious.[19] Still, it is also true that fathers almost always make an appearance in declamation because the possibility is recognized for their children to bring them to court for *dementia*; to contest before a judge an *abdicatio* considered unjust; to claim some unjust or inappropriate exercise of power, having one's case heard and one's reasons possibly accepted by the virtual court where *controversiae* are debated. Certainly, the school themes are structurally open—in the sense that the debates they stage never reach a conclusion that gives victory to one or the other party. But there are many declamations that mention in the theme cases of fathers who have tried many times to disinherit a child, but had the judges reject their application in each case (as in Seneca, *Controversia* 7.3, or in Pseudo-Quintilian's *Maior* 17). Thus, the possibility that the weaker party could defeat the stronger party in court was fully contemplated. Indeed, the very existence of a tribunal tasked with judging the legitimacy of disinheritance presupposes this possibility.

Charges of *dementia* plays a similar role. This is the only charge that in declamatory jurisprudence a child can bring against a father, as the theme of *Minor* 346 explains and as the following cases exemplify:

> A tyrant allows slaves to kill their masters and rape their mistresses. The city's nobles flee to foreign territory, and among these is one who has a son and a

---

18 Eco (1994), 101.
19 Breij (2016), 31.

daughter. While all the other slaves raped their mistresses, this man's slave respected the girl's virginity. When the tyrant is killed, the nobles return and crucify their slaves. This man instead frees his slave and gives him his daughter in marriage. The man is accused by his son of madness.[20]

Let a rapist, unless he is granted pardon within thirty days both by his father and by that of the woman he has assaulted, be condemned to death. A man commits rape. He is pardoned by the woman's father, but not by his own. He accuses his father of madness.[21]

The father of a *luxuriosus* fought heroically. He does not choose a prize as allowed to him by law. He is accused by his son of madness.[22]

A man, who had one frugal one and one *luxuriosus* son, disinherits the latter because he fell in love with a courtesan. The disinherited son moves in with the courtesan. When he falls ill, he summons his father and entrusts to him the child he has had by the courtesan, begging him to accept the child within the family. He dies. The old man wishes to accept the child into the family; the other son accuses him of madness.[23]

The *controversiae* on madness have recently been studied within the perspective of ancient medicine and of jurisprudence on mental illness, showing that declamation was again highly receptive to contemporary debates of science and learning, which were promptly echoed in the arguments of the rhetoricians.[24]

Besides precise references to this or that pathology or aetiology of psychological disfunction, what counts is that paternal behaviours can be challenged when they appear to be irrational or out of sync with the functions and duties of a father. As appears from the examples given here, the accusation of madness

---

20 Seneca, *Controversia* 7.6: Tyrannus permisit servis dominis interemptis dominas suas rapere. Profugerunt principes civitatis; inter eos qui filium et filiam habebat profectus est peregre. Cum omnes servi dominas suas vitiassent, servos eius virginem servavit. Occiso tyranno reversi sunt principes; in crucem servos sustulerunt. Ille manu misit et filiam conlocavit. Accusatur a filio dementiae.
21 Pseudo-Quintilian, *Declamationes minores*, 349: RAPTOR, NISI ET SUUM PATREM EXORAVERIT ET RAPTAE INTRA TRIGINTA DIES, PEREAT. Rapuit quidam. Exoravit patrem raptae, suum non exoravit. Dementiae accusat.
22 Pseudo-Quintilian, *Declamationes minores*, 367: Luxuriosi pater fortiter fecit. Praemium non optavit ex lege. Dementiae reus fit a filio.
23 Calpurnius Flaccus 30: Qui habebat filios frugi et luxuriosum, <luxuriosum> ob amore<m> meretricis abdicavit. Abdicatus se ad meretricem contulit. Illic cum aegrotare coepisset, misit ad patrem et commendavit illi filium de meretrice susceptum rogans, ut eum in familiam recipiat, et obiit. Vult illum senex in familiam recipere. Reus est alteri filio dementiae.
24 Rizzelli (2014b and 2015).

is a very thin veil, almost explicitly a pretext for the real problem, which is how to define the correct behaviour of a parent. The fact that it can be a child who questions that behaviour (even if the child must first ask a tribunal to recognize the merits of its claims) is an extremely important datum. In rhetorical schools, students learned to speak *for* fathers as well as *against* them. Analogously, husbands certainly enjoy a position of pre-eminence within the conjugal pair, but a wife hardly lacks juridical mechanisms for asserting her rights. When divorced, she has at her disposal the generic charge of ingratitude, in cases where the matrimonial selection has been conceived as a benefit to the husband, and the more specific charges of unjustified divorce, and above all of *mala tractatio*.[25] As in the case of the charge of madness against fathers, mistreatment is also often a convenient vehicle for bringing to the attention of judges a very wide range of marital behaviours. It is interesting that this charge is often invoked when actions relating to children are at stake, for example in the last two *Maiores*, where a father kills his son suspected of an incestuous relation with his mother:

> *Legal action is allowed for mistreatment.* Suspecting him of having committed incest with his mother, a father tortures his son in a removed part of the house and kills him in the midst of these torments. The mother asks him what he learned from the son, and on his refusal she accuses him of mistreatment.[26]

The underlying idea—but often made explicit: for instance, in Pseudo-Quintilian's grim eighth *Maior*, on the ill twins—is that children and mother represent a cohesive unit, almost to the point that any behaviour by the father that is harmful to the integrity or well-being of the children is considered *ipso facto* mistreatment of the mother, who can then bring this behaviour to account in court. We can see this in a theme cited for didactic purposes in manuals, in this case in Fortunatianus's *Ars rhetorica* (1.15): "He killed three children on the basis of the law that allows a father to put his children to death without trial. His wife accuses him of mistreatment".[27] Rather than highlighting the limits of the mother's agency—she is allowed to intervene in the male arena of public speech and the court only for protecting her children (but not, for example, for controlling their conduct)—to conclude that school rhetoric once again confirms

---

25 On *mala tractatio* see Hömke (2002), 164–181; Breij (2006a), and now Breij (2015a), 60–70.
26 MALAE TRACTATIONIS SIT ACTIO. Speciosum filium, infamem, tanquam incestum cum matre committeret, pater in secreta parte domus torsit et occidit in tormentis. Interrogat illum mater, quid ex filio compererit; nolentem dicere malae tractationis accusat. The theme is common to both declamations.
27 1.15 (= 87, 13–14 Calboli Montefusco): tres filios lege indemnatorum occidit; reus est uxori malae tractationis.

and reinforces gender differences (thus Margaret Imber), it is worth noting that by this oblique and indirect route, which figures the abuses of the husband against his children as an act of disrespect against the mother, the mother can in fact challenge the exercise of *patria potestas*—the most untouchable of paternal prerogatives—openly in court, thus contributing to the contestation of power, its extension and its limits, that we have been speaking about.[28]

The numerous controversies about sexual violence offer a final example (one of the themes, of Seneca the Elder's *Controversia* 1.5, has been translated in Chapter 4).[29] In this case, scholastic laws attribute to the woman who has suffered *raptus* a power she could never have exercised in real life, that of choosing to spare the life of her violator or not (a decision that must in any case be expressed before the court: even in such situations, declamation subjects the woman's prerogatives to the guarantee of a third party). In her research, Graziana Brescia has shown that this power is often undermined by a father's attempt to influence the daughter's decision and to guide her in a direction conforming to his own interests rather than her wishes.[30] But this does not detract from the fact that once again a weak link in the social system—a woman, a daughter, a victim of violence—is recognized as having certain rights that, in this case, elevate her above the opposing party and the nuclear family to which she is normally and by law subordinate.

Further examples could be given, but the point is clear. Far from being a mere recapitulation of traditional culture and its models, declamation is a potent vehicle for questioning that culture. It does not teach to be and think like a Roman, as many have claimed. In the rhetorical schools, one learned—instead—to negotiate the set of rules and interdictions inherited from the past, bringing different and opposing rights into interaction, staging new interpretive possibilities of conventional solutions, putting traditional models to the test in extreme situations that help confirm them or recommend their reconsideration. The fact that these models are represented in declamation in the form of laws that either attribute some right (e.g., to kill a child without trial) or impose some responsibility (e.g., to support one's parents in need) does not have the effect of armouring them from discussion. In fact, those laws become the subject of an unending interpretive negotiation and are juxtaposed to other, different and often contradictory, laws. This requires the identification of priorities, the introduction of derogations, and interventions where juridical law-making does not provide regulation. Declamation is, by its nature, a celebration of relativism.

---

28 Cf. Imber (2011).
29 A summary of the material is given in Packman (1999).
30 See Brescia (2012 and 2015a).

No god intervenes authoritatively to decide wrong and right. No conventionally accepted system of *mores* is so untouchable that it escapes the process of continual redefinition of roles and prerogatives. There are no free zones, no forbidden areas of debate, no powers secure in a position of primacy. If there are no winners and no losers at the end of a controversy, this is because there were none at the beginning.

Declamation does not promote social revolution or the radical redistribution of authority, any more than Plautine comedy aims for a society marked by the dominance of clever slaves or the humiliation of avaricious fathers. To discourage such interpretations, there is—if nothing else—the fact that the educational system of which declamation is the spearpoint was open only to men, and to a socially homogeneous class. This acted as a firm guarantee of the existing order of things. Moreover, the world constructed by declamation is a deliberately and explicitly fictional universe, a cosmos made of words that lived and flourished only within the walls of the classroom, ceasing to exist beyond those walls. Even with this clarification, however, the rhetorical schools taught that being and thinking like a Roman is not monolithic—some univocal and predefined code that the student must simply imbibe; in short, that Roman cultural identity is not a *thing* but a *process*, multifaceted and multilayered, kaleidoscopic and open to manipulation.

Not everything is possible in declamation. There are situations and relationships that declamation never explores, conflicts that none of the surviving texts thematize, probably because they clash with cultural principles that were considered non-negotiable. But beyond this restricted perimeter of *impossibilia*, the freedom of creativity and discussion that the declaimers permitted to themselves—and imparted to their students—is total, and the extent of this freedom and of the mental openness that it presupposed and promoted cannot be underestimated. We simply cannot reduce the scholastic curriculum to an education in conformity and to passive recapitulation of existing thought. In this sense, declamation represents perhaps the most "political" cultural product of all Latin literature.

6

DECLAMATION AND LAW

As we see in Chapter 1, every declamation is introduced by one or more legal dispositions, or by what is presented as such. These dispositions are normally placed at the beginning of the theme and are aimed at establishing the juridical frame within which the situation unfolds and the prerogatives recognized for the parties in the case, or those to which they appeal to justify their own claims. Omitted mention of laws does not necessarily imply their absence. There is a series of laws that are tacitly presupposed, because they are assumed to be well known to the students who are called upon to undertake the controversy: for example, the *lex scholastica* that recognizes the father's right to inflict *abdicatio* on his own child, or the law that gives to the *rapta* the possibility of choosing between the death of her seducer or reparative marriage (the latter often alluded to summarily through the formula *lex raptarum*).

In other cases, laws are implicit not because they can be easily supplied by the declaimer, but because they pertain to the cultural background against which the *controversia* is situated. Thus, the well-known paternal right over life and death, *vitae necisque potestas*—an idiosyncratic characteristic of Roman culture—is explicitly mentioned only in the collection of Calpurnius Flaccus, reworded as *indemnatos liberos liceat occidere* (as in the theme of extract 45). In the other anthologies that have reached us, this law is alluded to without the themes ever making express mention of it. This circumstance is likely explained by the fact that in the Roman context, the right was so much part of the shared imagination and of socially recognized practices that its existence was taken for granted, without it being necessary to recall it expressly to the attention of students.

The vast corpus of scholastic laws, which from one century to the next tend to be repeated substantially identical, have for a long time raised the question of their relation to the actually practised law of the Roman world, a problem that is in turn closely connected to that of the function of declamatory training with a view to access to the legal professions. Careful evaluations of the corpus were conducted many times over the course of the twentieth century and more recently, but no consensus has ever been reached that is valid for the totality of the laws used by the rhetoricians.[1] If in many cases the legal principles do find correspondences in attested laws, in others declamatory teaching seems to be shaped by Greek law; most often, we are dealing with a kind of spurious jurisprudence, which holds only within the confines of Sophistopolis and thus risked creating difficulties for students and teachers when they were no longer within the well-protected boundaries of the classroom. From this spring reservations, expressed by Petronius, Quintilian or Tacitus and often repeated uncritically by modern scholars, about a curriculum that proposed situations to its users that they could scarcely expect to encounter once they had completed that curriculum and had taken up roles as patrons or as legal experts. Before testing the foundations of these reservations, however, we need to examine certain salient characteristics of scholastic jurisprudence in its entirety.

To begin with, Sophistopolis presents itself as an entirely "legalized" world, in the sense that law seems to regulate every aspect of life and of relationships for its litigious inhabitants, while there are very few situations left to private negotiation or to the exercise of non-legal powers and prerogatives. Relations between fathers and sons constitute, again, a privileged lens through which to view the issue. In the City of the Rhetoricians, the rights of a son are not entrusted to general appeals to *pietas*, but are codified in a series of laws. The duty to give nourishment to aged parents, under pain of imprisonment, or more broadly of assisting them in conditions of grave discomfort (respectively *Liberi parentes alant aut vinciantur* and *Liberi parentes in calamitate ne deserant*), of obeying fathers (as can be inferred from the fact that they can be disinherited if they do not), of abstaining from violence against them (punishment being the loss of the hands: *Qui patrem pulsaverit, manus ei praecidantur*) or of suing them in court for dementia, and so on.[2] Even gratitude is subjected in the school themes to precise legal doctrines, invoked to sanction ingratitude: if for Cicero the duty of reciprocating benefits belongs to the category of *officia* (and thus represents a moral duty whose violation brings harm to one's honour and reputation but is not legally prosecuted), and if for Seneca juridical regulation of ingratitude would be absurd because it would threaten the spontaneity inherent in the exchange of benefits and distinguishes it from more venal forms of reciprocity, declamation envisions a specific *actio ingrati*, which can

---

1 Cf. the catalogues of Langer (2007) and Wycisk (2008), including earlier bibliography. On declamatory laws cf. also Lentano (2014b); Breij (2015b); Rizzelli (2015 and 2019); Lentano (2021b), 191–196.
2 On the laws about *alimenta* or assistance in calamity cf. Zinsmaier (2009), 33–34; Santorelli (2014), 191–197; D'Amati (2017 and 2018); van Mal-Maeder (2018), 13–24; on a *controversia* about beating one's father see most recently Lentano (2021a).

be enforced in court against anyone who has not sufficiently compensated a service received.³

One important consequence of the extension of the legal net to cover virtually all situations of interpersonal and social relations is that the court becomes the only venue for enforcing one's rights or to contest some behaviour deemed illegitimate. Other forms of regulation recognized by declamation appear insufficient or constitute the mere premise of a true debate that unfolds before the city's judges. Interesting in this respect is Pseudo-Quintilian's *Minor* 300, in which a husband first gives his son the task of judging his mother, who is suspected of adultery, in a domestic context, and then, when the woman is acquitted, prosecutes her in court and obtains her condemnation. Thus, the possibility of a domestic trial, in which the job of ascertaining the guilt of a member of the family is assumed by other members, is not entirely excluded. But it is significant that the right of having the final say is given only to public court. Public courts are the only ones endowed with the required impartiality of a third party, whereas the *iudicium domesticum* can be undermined by affective considerations and by personal ties, as in the case of the mother and the son who is called upon to judge her. But this is not the only case where the inadequacies and limits of family justice are highlighted: Seneca's *Controversia* 7.1 insists on the same point, when a presumed patricide has been condemned in a domestic trial.

It is worth adding that a different area—still characterized by the requirement of impartiality—appears in the *controversiae* where an individual (usually a father) seeks authorization to take his own life, offering reasons for *voluntaria mors*. Declamatory practice imposes on the aspiring suicide a *prosangelia*, or "self-incrimination", with which he asks the authorities (in Latin *controversiae* normally corresponding to the Senate) to preventatively approve his act, under pain of remaining unburied.⁴ Besides the debate that such themes provoked in the context of rhetorical teaching—whether it was appropriate to use self-incrimination figuratively, not for obtaining authorization for suicide, but to bring attention to one's own unhappy condition and to cast blame on the counterparty responsible for it—what I want to highlight is how a public institution is called upon to make pronouncements on situations and conflicts that originate in the private sphere. The only scenario that does not belong among those described so far occurs in the third *Maior* of Pseudo-Quintilian, the *Miles Marianus*, a historical theme in which

---

3 Cf., respectively, Cicero, *De officiis*, 1.47 and Seneca, *De beneficiis*, 3.6–17, with explicit reference to the scholastic law in question; Seneca's *Controversiae* 2.5 and 9.2 are both based on *actio ingrati*.
4 The question is explored in Stramaglia (2013), 85; Brescia and Lentano (2020), 110–116.

the case of a soldier who has killed a tribune to escape the *stuprum* that the latter intended to carry out is judged in the camp of Gaius Marius, the great Republican general, engaged at that time in the campaign against the Cimbri. Not by chance, the declaimer called upon to defend the soldier's case insists more than once on the commander's duty of impartiality, a duty made all the more critical by the fact that the tribune was one of his relatives.[5] In short, what Sophistopolis taught its adherents was that the only regulatory principle of cohabitation is the law—and thus, concretely, the courts where it was enforced, as well as the declaimers, those future holders of public discourse and of authoritative speech, who guaranteed its correction application. And if this suggests the idea of a professional class that aims simply at promoting itself, at protecting its own role and its own social dignity, what actually emerges from a consideration of scholastic rhetoric is the idea that every judgment, every encroachment on the limits of rights, every abuse of authority is evaluated by a wise legislative system, sanctioned by an impartial jury and supervised by the holders of effective speech whose job is to protect that order: another element, then, of the "politics" of declamation.

Let us come now to the nub of the question, that of the relationship between school jurisprudence and real law, and thus between declamatory training and forensic practice. Given that the two contexts only very partially overlap, we need to ask whether this really invalidates the formative value of the rhetorical curriculum and renders it inadequate for accessing the roles of the imperial bureaucracy, for political activity and for the forensic professions, as ancient and modern detractors of declamation have often claimed. I believe not. Recent studies by Romanists such as Dario Mantovani, Marta Bettinazzi, Jakob Stagl, and Giunio Rizzelli have shown that, although declamatory laws are often fictitious, the arguments and reasoning developed by rhetoricians are completely in line and often perfectly in sync with the thinking of jurists of the classical period.[6] This is the case of the much-discussed thirteenth *Maior* of Pseudo-Quintilian, *The poor man's bees*:

> *Causing malicious damage is to be actionable.* A poor man and a rich man were neighbours in the country, and their gardens adjoined each other. The rich man had flowers in his garden, the poor man kept bees in his. The rich man complained that his flowers were being browsed on by the poor man's bees. He gave him notice to move them. When the poor man failed to do so, the

---

5   Cf. Bernstein (2013b), 21–32. The theme recurs also in the third extract of Calpurnius Flaccus.
6   Cf. respectively Mantovani (2007 and 2014); Bettinazzi (2012 and 2014); Stagl (2012); Rizzelli (2014b and 2015).

rich man sprinkled poison over his flowers. The poor man's bees all died. The rich man is accused of causing malicious damage.[7]

This declamation is not only inspired by a well attested Roman law, the *lex Aquilia de damno*, but also spells out a problem of *ius controversum* addressed by theory, that of the ownership of animals, who by their nature tend to wander from their own land. Jurisprudence states that ownership obtains only so long as the animals exhibit *animus revertendi*, namely an intention (or habit) of returning home. In the theoretical debate, the question centred precisely on bees, in order to establish if the principle of *animus revertendi* could be applied in their case as well (as it did to doves, for example), or if they must be considered "owned" only to the extent that they were physically under the control of the owner. Apparently, the principle of *animus revertendi* was considered to hold in the case of bees, but the question must have been sufficiently interesting to motivate its appearance in Pseudo-Quintilian's *controversia*, which can be attributed to a rhetorician of sound juridical education, as he "stages" the terms of the debate in the form of a concrete scenario.

The situation is similar for much more "technical" texts, such as *Minor* 260, *A mother-in-law and daughter-in-law in a fight over dowries*, whose valuable juridical argumentation is worthy of a jurist and constitutes an important source for the reconstruction of dowry law; or *Minor* 302, *A gladiator to bury his father*, which is influenced by theoretical debates over the status of gladiators and *scaenici*. Further examples could be given. Certainly, the idea is somewhat one-sided that when rhetorical argumentation and doctrinal reflection seem to touch in some way, this must be due to the influence of the latter on the former. In fact, in some cases it is possible or indeed probable that it was the declaimers who influenced the debates of jurisprudence, and not the other way around. Moreover, we cannot forget that the jurists themselves were trained in the rhetorical schools, and in many cases this training left an indelible imprint on their activities as interpreters of the law or as members of the imperial chancellery (as Jakob Stagl has recently emphasized).[8]

An interesting example from this point of view is constituted by the *controversiae* on adultery.[9] These controversies amount to about a tenth of the entire

---

7 DAMNI PER INIURIAM DATI SIT ACTIO. Pauper et dives in agro vicini erant iunctis hortulis. Habebat dives in horto flores, pauper apes. Questus est dives flores suos decerpi ab apibus pauperis. Denuntiavit ut transferret. Illo non transferente flores suos veneno sparsit. Apes pauperis omnes perierunt. Reus est dives damni iniuria dati. Besides the authors cited in the previous note, see also Corbino (2009); Desanti (2015), 175ff.
8 Cf. Stagl (2012). For another example of declamation (possibly) influencing imperial jurisprudence see Rizzelli (2021).
9 Brescia and Lentano (2016), 135–184.

corpus of preserved themes. In that light, what is striking is that on a key point—the law punishing lovers caught in the act—the declaimers seem deliberately to ignore the *lex Iulia de adulteriis coercendis*, the measure approved by Augustus between 18 and 16 BCE that remained in force up to the period of Justinian, and which was the subject of countless interpretations whose traces can be seen even in the drastic reduction made by the editors of the *Digest*. If the legislative regime launched by the *princeps* rigorously restricted *ius occidendi* to the father of the woman and removed it from the husband (except in very well-defined circumstances), declamation instead adopted a version of that law that, with minimal differences in its wording, recommends death for the two lovers and recognizes the right of *anyone* who has caught them in the act to exact this punishment, in the first instance the husband: "Whosoever surprises an adulterer together with the adulteress, provided that he has killed both, will not be culpable" (thus Seneca's *Controversia* 1.4, whose theme we have translated in Chapter 1, and 9.1).

The reasons behind such a choice on the part of the rhetoricians are not easy to identify. According to the conventional interpretation, they were inspired by the legal regime that preceded the Augustan law, which had recognized the husband's right to avenge his violated honour, but this is an assertion rather than an explanation. Nor is the hypothesis of passive imitation of Greek law persuasive, since at least in the context we know best—Athens—similar laws did not permit the killing of the adulterous woman. We are thus warranted in posing the question in new terms, revealing different aspects of the *controversiae* on adultery. If the Augustan law as such appears foreign to the rhetoricians, the school texts—and in particular Pseudo-Quintilian's *Minores*—strongly emphasize the motif of *iustus dolor*, "legitimate resentment", affecting the husband when he has caught an adulterer *in flagrante delicto* and justifies the passionate reaction that leads to the death of the two lovers:[10]

> This law [the one permitting the husband to punish his wife and her lover] was written in view of the grief experienced by the husband, and that famous creator and extender of the law wished it to be exercised privately [i.e., that it did not require the intervention of the public tribunal].[11]

Now, this is important because it finds precise reflection in imperial interventions datable to the Antonine age that were aimed at mitigating, in consideration

---

10 For other cases, cf. Graziana Brescia's section in Brescia and Lentano (2016); cf. also Brescia (2019b).
11 Cf. 277.3 (one of the possible examples): Hoc ius scriptum est mariti dolori, hoc ius ille conditor conscriptorque legis huius voluit esse privatum. Cf. Brescia (2019a).

of *iustus dolor*, the strictness of the *lex Iulia* in punishing a husband who had executed his adulterous wife in order to redress the damage she had brought upon the integrity of the *domus*.[12] This is the case of a rescript of Antoninus Pius, according to whom a husband who admits to having killed his wife caught *in flagrante delicto* can be acquitted of a capital charge insofar as "it is extremely difficult to rein in one's own legitimate grief".[13]

In cases like this, evaluating the relationship (if any) between laws of the imperial chancellery and declamatory practice is not easy. If the rescript of Antoninus Pius is the most ancient pronouncement on weakening the *lex Iulia* (as seems reasonable to assume from the fact that the juridical sources do not report earlier interventions), it is chronologically later than the redaction of the *Minores*, which if are not the work of Quintilian himself (who died in 96 CE), nevertheless can be attributed to one of his students and thus can be dated to the beginning of the second century CE. We can say, then, that the theme of *iustus dolor* must have been "in the air" and that probably both declamation and imperial jurisprudence drew on the same lively debate at the turn of the second century and a sensibility that was maturing vis-à-vis customary behaviours—or, if we prefer, a lasting resistance to introducing novelties around *ius occidendi* by Augustan legislation in respect to Republican legislation. If declamation is not a direct inspiration for legislative proposals or doctrinal clarifications, it is nevertheless a participant in the same cultural milieu in which both mature, thanks again to the rhetorical training that almost all the jurists would have had, and which in many cases will have influenced their later exegetical activities.

But beyond the frequent affinity that the logic and practice of rhetoricians show with that of jurists, there is, in my view, a deeper level at which declamation and the law come together. Paying too much attention to the contents of the school laws and to examining their correspondences with laws actually attested in surviving codices risks overlooking something crucial: the cognitive abilities and mental habits of those who undertook rhetorical training in their formative years. I have already mentioned the idea of the primacy of the law and of the court as the *only* site for negotiating social and family conflicts. But there is something else. The majority of the *controversiae* we possess play out along two dimensions: on the one hand, the definition of the action under discussion, and on the other the clarification of the laws that guide this discussion and verification of their applicability to the case in question. (These two aspects may co-exist within the

---

12 Ample documentation in Rizzelli (2014a), 283–299, with occasional reference also to the school *controversiae*.

13 *Digesta*, 48.5.39(38).8: Ei, qui uxorem suam in adulterio deprehensam occidisse se non negat, ultimum supplicium remitti potest, cum sit difficillimum iustum dolorem temperare.

same declamation, of course.) Texts of the first type fall under the so-called *status finitivus*, where what is at stake is a shared definition of the behaviour of one of the two parties—whether the relationship can correctly be called "adultery" between a woman and a man who until recently had been her husband; whether it is legal to call the killing of a despot for purely personal defence "tyrannicide"; and so on. In such cases, the fictitious nature of the law that sparks the discussion or the more or less improbable character of the situation that justifies it are much less important than the form in which the discussion is conducted and the analytical skills that it helps sharpen: forms and skills that can then be applied to complex laws and situations from the real world. The same reasoning holds for the second type of texts we have mentioned, those that belong, according to the ancient terminology, under the rubric of "contradiction" (apparent or real) between the letter of the law and the legislator's intention, or between different laws, and so belong to the category of *status legales*. Here, too, the spurious character of the juridical text on which discussion turns is entirely irrelevant to the skills that one needs to interpret that text.

As Petronius's *Satyricon* remarks, when declaimers finally landed in the forensic context, they may have had impression of being in *terra incognita*: a world in which the familiar, habitual themes and characters of declamation were gone, replaced by radically different forms of interaction with the public and with the opposing party. In that context, the obligations and interdictions of praetors awaited them, rather than wizards, plagues, oracular responses, or stepmothers crueller than those of tragedy, as Quintilian (2.10.5) put it. In the schools, everything was simple. In the Forum, "we must examine documents, testimony, contracts, agreements, obligations, relationships of blood and of acquisition, decrees and responses".[14] Nevertheless, graduates of the rhetorical schools had extensive training in confronting an articulated system of juridical laws (even if simplified) and had developed an aptitude for discussing the individual concrete case (even if improbable) by contextualizing it within that system. Whether the laws at the heart of some *controversia* were real or fictitious, what counts is the intellectual habits they presupposed—and helped shaping. Confronted with the law of a declamatory theme, the student was urged to question the applicability of abstract law to the concrete case in question, to define its extension and limits, to examine the intention of the legislator behind the literal words of a text that might sometimes be vague or ambiguous, to hypothesize possible exceptions, and so on. He learned to move within a complex legal system, where two laws could be conflictual and whose combination

---

14 Cicero, *De oratore*, 2.100.

might lead to consequences both unexpected and unacceptable. The fact that—especially from the beginning of the second century CE—legal innovations often came about through imperial rescripts (alongside the more traditional *responsa* of jurists) and that these often gave responses to individual cases often as intricate as any school theme, must have made rhetorical training even more relevant to the activities of the interpreters of law.

If my reading of the controversies is correct, it follows that in spite of the perplexity expressed by many in this regard, the schools of rhetoric did in fact adequately perform the task they were called upon to do by those who frequented them. And this means their critics have been wrong to focus on the most showy and also most superficial manifestations of that world, missing the deeper significance of rhetorical training. Behind all the severe or overly indulgent fathers, all the cruel stepmothers, all the pirates and bloody tyrants, all the ghosts and phantasms, all the sublime heroism or petty villainy, what they were talking about was real questions of power and wealth, of justice and equality, of good and bad politics, of the flexibility of the law and the power of the word. Out of all the overblown discourse, all the verbiage meant for effect, all the literary allusion, there comes—forcefully—a notion of the law as the *only* foundation for civil co-existence, and a rejection of any prerogative that claims to be above or free from the law entirely, whether this prerogative is claimed by a father, a tyrant, or a *vir fortis*. To understand this, and to appreciate the contribution that the school *controversiae* give to our understanding of ancient culture through its development over the course of the imperial age, it is sufficient to go deeper than the "poppy-seed and sesame" of their words.

7

GREEKS AND ROMANS

Before opening this chapter, we must recall the caveat given in the Introduction. A comparative study of Greek and Roman declamation is both desirable and warranted, since declamation involves the western and eastern halves of the empire equally, to the point that any partial analysis of this *koiné* would be *ipso facto* artificial. However, research of this kind is beyond the scope of this volume and is still forthcoming. What a succinct introduction to the phenomenon of school rhetoric can do is to offer some *specimina* of the problem, with the aim of revealing not only the elements that shared between Greek and Roman *controversiae*, but also the divergences, differences, and dissimilarities between them, to the extent it is possible to trace these to the different cultural sensibilities of the rhetoricians belonging to the two great macro-areas into which the Roman world was divided.

Initial, illuminating proof of the different sensibilities of Greek and Roman declaimers, even though involved in managing a largely shared set of themes, is offered by Seneca the Elder.[1] Let us consider the theme of *Controversia* 1.8, which has been translated in Chapter 1: a *vir fortis* who has distinguished himself in war three times wishes to return to battle a fourth time, notwithstanding his father's prohibition and the existence of a law that exempts those who have heroically fought three times from *militia* (This is the figure of the *ter fortis*, less frequent in the surviving collections, corresponding to the Greek *trisaristeús*). As we can imagine, at the son's refusal to renounce his new battle commission, the father disinherits the young hero.

In the section related to *divisio*—that line-up of topics to be covered that constitutes, according to the metaphor used by the schools, the "bones" of the entire *controversia*—Seneca informs us that all the declaimers proposed treating the question whether a son could even be disinherited if he had availed himself of a power granted to him by law (a *quaestio vulgaris*, as Seneca says, applicable generically to a wide range of different themes). Above all, paternal *abdicatio* punished not only illegal behaviours, but also the lack of filial *officia* towards the

---

1 Cf. now Guérin (2018 and 2020).

father, coinciding in this case with the lack of obedience. More interesting is the observation expressed immediately after, in the first person by Seneca himself:

> Greeks propose, initially, a question that turns out to be intolerable to Roman sensibilities: whether it is legal to disinherit a *vir fortis*. I do not see what rationale could be given to justify a negative response. The circumstance of a *vir fortis*—and in this case one who, moreover, has fought heroically many times—grants him greater title to merits, but not greater rights.[2]

Seneca frequently refers to Greek declaimers en bloc, as if they constituted a compact and homogeneous group in the panorama of teachers heard by him.[3] In this case, Seneca informs us that in the *controversiae* about disinheritance of a *vir fortis*, Greek declaimers were accustomed to question the legality of the father's action. In this case, disinheritance applied to a son who had done well by the collective and by his family, which was the inevitable beneficiary of his prestige. Among other things, we have here confirmation of this position, though chronologically much later than Seneca's anthology, in the text of a declamation of Libanius, the teacher of Antioch close to the emperor Julian, where an *aristeús* disinherited by his father raises as an objection the non-applicability to war heroes of *apokéryxis*, the Greek equivalent of Roman *abdicatio*.[4]

Seneca's refutation of this argumentative strategy is swift. "Roman sensibilities" would not tolerate an imposition of this kind, in the sense that it appeared unacceptable to the particular cultural sensibility of Latin rhetoricians. Warlike *virtus*—the author argues—confers a *plus commendationis*, not a *plus iuris*: it does not influence the legal status of the son, that is, his subordination to the authority of his father, and thus does not impinge in any way on the father's ability to exercise the prerogative of *abdicatio* against him. The position of a son is defined by law and by custom and has nothing to do with individual merits, however great these may be. One can discuss the greater or lesser reasonableness of the disownment, its timeliness, but the legality of the father availing himself of this tool remains unquestionable.

In the same *Controversia* 1.8, there is another interesting passage. Among the positions of the rhetoricians who defend the father, Seneca cites that of the Greek declaimer Aeschines, in part translating his words into Latin, and in part—and

---

2 1.8.7: Graeci illam quaestionem primam solent temptare, quam Romanae aures non ferunt: an vir fortis abdicari possit. Non video autem, quid adlaturi sint, quare non possit, nam quod et vir fortis est et totiens fortiter fecit, non plus iuris illi adfert, sed plus commendationis.
3 Cf. Citti (2007); Echavarren (2007). On quotations from Greek declaimers in Seneca cf. now Citti (2018).
4 *Declamationes*, 33.29–30, on which see Johansson (2015), 275.

on the crucial point—leaving them in Greek (in the translation I have left in italics the words that Seneca cites in Greek):

> I don't care about glory—this is not what makes me more desirous of being with you—nor do I care about that courage of yours that is the envy of all. I want to explain, fully, my feelings as a father—each can interpret them as he wishes: *I will love him this much even if he behaves as a knave.*[5]

Seneca comments on these words first in an impersonal form ("We had the impression that Aeschines, to express the indulgent attitude of the father, had compromised his dignity"), then entrusts to his spokesman, the rhetorician Porcius Latro, the idea that a father would be preferred who was "guided by rational rather than emotional considerations".[6] Called into question by Aeschines's words are key values of the Roman military code such as *gloria* and *virtus*, which the father claimed to place below his desire to enjoy his son's company and to keep him safe from the risks of a new war: an "egoistic" and, evidently in the judgement of Latro, an irrational interest that ended up harming the very *dignitas* of the father, obfuscating his role as mediator of the axiological system in which the entire collective sees itself reflected.

The distance between Greek and Latin teachers suggested by 1.8, as observed by Janet Fairweather, recalls a very similar case in the preceding *controversia* in Seneca's anthology, whose theme has also been translated in Chapter 1.[7] It features a father who refuses to ransom his son from pirates after this son had killed his two brothers, the first a tyrant, the second an adulterer with his (the son's) wife. The son is then spontaneously released by pirates and, in turn, refuses to maintain his father after he (the father) has fallen on hard times. Here, Seneca mentions Greek rhetoricians again, still treated as a homogeneous group, and refers to an "incorrect question" raised by them: whether a father can avail himself, against a tyrannicidal son, of a law that punishes by imprisonment those who have not maintained his own parents, here cited in the form "Children shall maintain their parents, or be placed in chains", and present in many declamations with only minor differences:

> It will be enough to mention one or two occasions, in *controversiae* of this kind, when an incorrect question is posed by the Greeks: whether it is legal

---

5   1.8.11: non me gloria cupidiorem tui fecit, non omnibus admiranda virtus, "confitebor" inquit "adfectus patris, quos ut quisque volet interpretetur: οὕτως ἂν καὶ δειλὸν ἐφίλουν".
6   1.8.11: Videbatur hic, dum indulgentiam exprimit, non servasse dignitatem patris. Placebat autem Latroni potius ratione retinere patrem quam affectu.
7   Fairweather (1981), 115 and 153.

for a father to avail himself of this law against a tyrannicide. Those hands, they say, are in a certain sense sacred and public, to the point that not even pirates believed they had rights regarding them. Ours do not even consider questions like this.[8]

This is essentially a variation of the preceding case, not only because the *vir fortis* and the tyrannicide are very similar figures—sharing full discretion in the choice of their reward—but also because in both passages the possibility of a father exercising his prerogatives against a son of such exceptional merits (as he would against any son in any circumstance) is debated, with the further idea that it would be particularly impious to deny liberty to hands that have restored liberty to all citizens (to the point that even pirates, the bearers par excellence of *vincula* in the universe of Sophistopolis, respect this principle).

In this case, the Greek thesis consisted of affirming that the hands of the tyrannicide are "sacred and public". In some way, they, and the person they belong to, acquire the status of a collective inheritance, or even a good consecrated to the gods, whose availability is removed from those exercising a purely "private" and human authority like the father's over them. As can be seen, Seneca limits himself to mentioning that Roman declaimers do not consider such questions, without specifying the reasons for this refusal, and this notwithstanding that the expression "public hands" actually occurs in some texts of Latin rhetoricians reported by Seneca himself (so Latro in 1.7.1). These reasons can nevertheless be deduced by comparison with the parallel case in 1.8. While Greek rhetoricians considered the merits acquired by children established for their benefit a "rule of exception", which exempted them from paternal authority, their Latin colleagues considered that position unacceptable or simply incomprehensible. In their rejection of the question raised by Greeks, we see again the conditioned reflexes of a culture in which paternal *potestas* has its own unique profile, lacking parallels in other and different contexts.

In this perspective, another interesting aspect—and one relevant to the motif of the conflict between father and sons—is the observation that has been made in some recent contributions on the declamations of Libanius that in Greek rhetoric disinheritance is invariably represented as a measure that must be authorized by a jury (see, e.g., *Declamation* 33.23) or even by the *boulé*, the ancient council of Athenian democracy (as in *Declamation* 27.2), and that the father cannot

---

8   1.7.12: Graecorum improbam quaestionem satis erit in eiusmodi controversiis semel aut iterum adnotasse: an in tyrannicidam uti pater hac lege possit: quasi sacras et publicas manus esse, in quas sibi ne piratae quidem licere quicquam putent. Nostri hoc genus quaestionis submoverunt.

exercise on his own initiative.[9] By contrast, in Latin declamations fathers inflict *abdicatio* on their children without the permission of any public institution, with immediate effect, except in cases where the *abdicatus* brings a complaint to the tribunal. Does such a difference derive from the characteristics of *apokéryxis*, the punitive measure that in the Greek context corresponds to Latin *abdicatio*? Our information is very fragmentary. According to Alick Harrison, whose manual is still one of the more authoritative reconstructions of Athenian juridical reality, there is no evidence that the father was required to take a case of disinheritance before a judge, nor that the child had the right to appeal. Even the need to consult with other members of the family is unproven. This is mandatory in Plato's imagined city in the *Laws*, but it is impossible to establish to what degree Plato reworked historical legislation actually in force in Athens.[10] What is certain—because it can be inferred from the Greek term—is that the father's decision had to be announced to the city through public banns (a herald: *kéryx*). This requirement is missing in the Roman world, and this explains why of the two verbs used in Greek to indicate disinheritance, *apeîpon* (and its variants) and *apokerútto*, only the former has a precise equivalent in Latin (*abdico*). Declamation is not, for the most part, called into question in examining this issue;[11] and yet the decision of a tribunal as the condition of disinheritance is affirmed in Lucian's *Bis abdicatus* (8), two centuries before Libanius, where this decision serves to prevent the father acting on impulses of anger or under the influence of slander. In the Latin controversies, there are occasionally traces of *consilium necessariorum*, the informal meeting of family and friends that a father could convene in preparing to impose punishment against his child (*Minor* 356.2), but normally *abdicatio* is the outcome of an autonomous paternal decision. It is difficult not to think that this situation is tied up with the value of Roman *patria potestas* in respect to a Greek father's corrective powers, which probably would have made the need to seek a public body's agreement simply incomprehensible to a Latin audience.

The different treatment of the relationship between father and sons in Greek and Roman rhetoricians suggests another example. I have already mentioned the case of *Minor* 326, in which a son kills himself publicly after the oracle fingers him as a sacrificial victim required to stop a plague, and notwithstanding his father's attempts to save him. Here we can add that the theme of Pseudo-Quintilian finds an exact correspondence in a declamation of Sopatros, active in Athens during the fourth century CE, the author of a collection of school themes, the *Quaestionum divisio*, which in certain respects represents the Greek

---

9   Johansson (2006), 66–69 and (2015); and cf. Schouler (1984), vol. 2, 858A.
10 Harrison (2001), vol. 1, 80–81 and n. 58.
11 But cf. Piccirilli (1981), 353.

complement of the *Minores* (n. 40 in the recent edition of Weißenberger). Even a quick glance indicates that Sopatros attributed greater importance to the father's feelings than Pseudo-Quintilian did, imagining among other things that the young man chosen for sacrifice was an only son—a point that is absent in the theme—and portraying the father inconsolable at the prospective loss of his only heir and of support in his old age. In the Greek rhetorician's text, the father's love for his son is presented in fact as a sort of inescapable restriction, a *force majeure*, the expression of a *phýsis* shared by all men and that for this reason can entreat the indulgence of the court before which the accused is brought. A similar accentuation of the affective dimension was instead considered by Roman declaimers to be harmful to paternal *dignitas*, as emerges from Seneca's *Controversia* 1.8, mentioned earlier, and in fact there is no trace of it in the parallel development of Pseudo-Quintilian, where the father actually seems pleased by the son's heroism in not refusing to die for his city, and whose story, for this reason, is destined to be counted as material for *exempla*.

In some cases, the different sensibility of Roman rhetoricians in respect to their Greek colleagues emerges not so much in their different approach to the same theme, but, so to speak, *ex silentio*, in the sense that we can draw conclusions from the absence of a specific *argumentum* in the Latin themes in respect to the Greek context. Such absences could, of course, be owing to the caprice of the manuscript tradition—which deprives us, we must remember, of almost 250 minor declamations—or to the partiality of the preserved material. But at least in certain cases, we can suppose that this absence is the result of specific choices on the part of Latin teachers, who considered some themes unfit for the cultural context in which they operate. Let's consider a single example.

In the *Division of Questions* written by Sopatros the rhetorician, the case of a mother who kills her son in a gymnasium where he had sought refuge is presented. In killing her son, she violated the law that prohibits women from entering gymnasia, conceived in Greek culture as an exclusively male place (70, 219 Weißenberger):

> *The woman who enters in a gymnasium should be punished by death. It should be permissible for mothers to kill their children without due process.* A mother, whose son was prostituting himself, followed him with the intention of killing him. The son got ahead and took refuge in the gymnasium. The mother entered and then killed her son within the gymnasium. She is charged on legal grounds.

The Roman world did not have any institution corresponding precisely to the Greek gymnasium; however, the motif occurs also in the Latin manuals. Quintilian, to exemplify the case of two laws that contradict one another, cited the law that prohibited putting statues of women in a palaestra, along with that requiring the placement of the statues of tyrannicides in palaestras, when there was the case of a female tyrannicide (7.7.5). The incompatibility between the male-only space of the gymnasium and the tyrannicide's gender is so strong that it extends even to statues, when it is the mere image of a female figure that "enters" that space.

But there is something else. In the theme proposed by Sopatros, a second law appears, entirely lacking Roman parallels. According to this law, mothers are permitted to kill their children without due process. To tell the truth, the Greek expression used by Sopatros—*ákritoi paîdes*—does find an equivalent in the phrase *indemnati liberi*, sometimes attested in the Latin collections. But in no Roman *controversia* is this right ever given to mothers. In texts where it occurs, the formula *indemnatos liberos liceat occidere* does not even require a complementary term that explains *for whom* the right is recognized; in Roman society, the only ones who could exercise this right to kill are fathers, and a law like the one mentioned by Sopatros cannot be found—if I am not mistaken—either in the surviving Latin collections or in the rhetorical manuals.

Finally, the Greek declaimers were generally viewed as more open to sordid themes, which staged scabrous situations and involved the use of obscene terms and images.[12] This attitude can be seen in Seneca's aforementioned *Controversia* 1.2, relating to the woman kidnapped by pirates, handed over to a pimp, and now applying to be a priestess—a theme that lends itself very well to irony about the woman's claim to have maintained her chastity despite both her long stay in a brothel and among the pirates. In the final section of the controversy, where forensic examination often yields to digression and anecdote, Seneca briefly mentions a similar theme, that of the woman who accuses her husband of maltreatment following an unconsummated marriage, wins his condemnation, and then applies a priesthood. In *that* case, he recalls an unnamed rhetorician (he says only that it is an ex-praetor) who had maliciously alluded to husbands "playing nearby" on the first night of marriage, out of respect for the virginity of their timid wives, adding that according to Mamercus Aemilius Scaurus the predilection for obscenity "was learned from the Greek declaimers, who granted themselves every license".[13] Almost to exemplify what he has just said, Seneca

---

12 On this point, cf. Longo (2016).
13 1.2.22: Hoc genus sensus memini quondam praetorium dicere, cum declamaret controversias de illa, quae egit cum viro malae tractationis, quod virgo esset, et damnavit; postea petit sacerdotium: novimus, inquit, istam maritorum abstinentiam, qui, etiamsi primam virginibus timidis remisere noctem, vicinis tamen locis ludunt. [...] Hoc autem vitium aiebat Scaurus a Graecis declamatoribus tractum, qui nihil et non permiserint sibi et +penetraverunt+.

cites another controversy in which a husband catches his wife in adultery not with another man but with a woman, reporting some rather salty utterances of Greek declaimers and concluding with the trenchant affirmation that "some things are better left unsaid with harm to the case than spoken with harm to modesty".[14]

Scholarly reconstructions of the theme alluded to by Seneca are not univocal. At base, there must be the husband's right to kill his wife and her lover caught *in flagrante delicto*, according to the time-honoured declamatory law discussed in Chapter 6. Here, however, the scenario is made more complex by the fact that the adulterous relationship was of a homosexual kind. It is possible, therefore, that the theme envisioned a problem of *finitio*—whether, that is, the sexual relationship between two women could be defined as "adultery". Alluding to lesbian relationships, Martial speaks of a "riddle" more obscure than that of the Sphinx, which states that "where there is no man, there is adultery".[15] Alternatively, the case may deal with the *status* of the conflict between the legislator's intention and the letter of the law, which regarding the husband's right to kill the lover only speaks of an "adulterer" and "adulteress" (or, more often, of "adulterers", masculine). In both cases, then, these are questions that are broadly addressed by extant *controversiae*. But it is telling that the idea raised by Seneca remains entirely isolated and that no preserved Latin declamation turns on themes of lesbian love. Thus, we probably have one of those situations in which "what conditioned the fortune of the declamatory themes was the ethical-moral reservations that their subjects could possibly provoke".[16] In this case, however, such reservations have a precise cultural manifestation, in the sense that they refer to tastes characterized as specifically Greek (even if they influenced Latin declaimers as well, in Seneca's view negatively and requiring distancing from). Furthermore, Quintilian, when he confronts the question of obscene terms in school themes, appeals again to *pudor*, and very precisely to what he calls *Romani pudoris mos*, "traditional Roman modesty"—an expression in which the adjective counts at least as much as the noun (8.3.39).[17]

We can conclude this chapter by recalling other important differences between Greek and Latin declamation, in the choice of themes or in their

---

14 1.1.23: Longe recedendum est ab omni obscenitate et verborum et sensuum; quaedam satius est causae detrimento tacere quam verecundiae dicere. Close analysis of these two Senecan passages, and of the significant interpretive problems they present, in Citti (2007), 75–81; cf. also Longo (2016); Rolle (2018).
15 Martial 1.90.9–10: Commenta es dignum Thebano aenigmate monstrum, / hic ubi vir non est, ut sit adulterium.
16 Stramaglia (2015), 154.
17 Cf. Fairweather (1981), 196.

formulation. The presence of *controversiae* on the figure of the stepmother is much more abundant in Latin, probably because of the particular characteristics of the Roman *familia* and its related matrimonial practices. In Greek rhetoric, the conflict between rich and poor is loaded with political and ideological meanings, such as the linkage between wealth and aspirations to tyranny, typical of Athenian democratic reflection; by contrast, this aspect is almost entirely absent in the Roman context. Greek declamation gives much space to historical themes, which in Latin constitute a very small minority (confirmed also by papyrological finds).[18] Moreover, Greek rhetoricians seem to focus exclusively on the age of Athenian hegemony, on confrontation with the growing power of Macedonia, and on the saga of Alexander the Great, whereas their Latin colleagues prefer events of recent history, even touching on "hot" and potentially dangerous political themes. In my view, no convincing explanation has yet been given for this difference, but it has an important *pendant* in Plutarch's choices of Greek protagonists for his *Parallel Lives*. Lucia Pasetti has recently illustrated overlaps as well as divergences between Greek and Latin declamations about poisoning, a theme that in the Roman context does not need to await school rhetoric before rising to the attention of judicial chroniclers and historiographers.[19] Pasetti has also shown how differently the philosopher is represented in Greek *controversiae*—where he is almost invariably a positive figure of great individual morality—and in Latin texts, in some of which the practice of philosophy is seen as unreconcilable with traditional Roman *mores*.[20]

Regarding style, which is also a sort of identity claim, in *Controversia* 2.6, Seneca reports, in Greek, a *sententia* of Agroitas of Marseille, and then adds that this declaimer expressed himself "with rough technique, from which it was inferred that he had not been among Greeks, but with strong expressions, from which it was inferred that he had been among Romans".[21] The juxtaposition between the refined grace of Greek and the less elaborate but more robust eloquence of Latin is certainly not an invention of Seneca the Elder, but the observation is important. When Livy had made his Mucius Scaevola say that *et facere et pati fortia Romanum est*, he was voicing a trait of Roman identity (2.12.9). In the Senecan anthology, the stress moves from action to speech, underlining that it is no less "Roman" *dicere fortia*.

---

18   Cribiore (2001), 233–238.
19   Cf. Pasetti (2015).
20   Pasetti (2016).
21   2.6.12: Dicebat autem Agroitas arte inculta, ut scires illum inter Graecos non fuisse, sententiis fortibus, ut scires illum inter Romanos fuisse.

Other aspects, traceable to their respective cultural frames, could be identified through further analysis.[22] But from the evidence given so far, we can conclude that declamations—notwithstanding their widespread distribution and the circulation of themes, motifs, and teachers from one side of the empire to the other—never entirely lose their connection with the cultural context in which they were elaborated. They reflect an imaginary that was in large part shared—but that also tends, in some cases, to articulate itself according to an easily identifiable "national" inflection.

---

22 E.g., Lentano (2014a).

BIBLIOGRAPHY

Amato, E., Citti, F., and Huelsenbeck, B. (eds), *Law and Ethics in Greek and Roman Declamation*, Berlin, Munich, and Boston.

Balbo, A. (2016), "Ri-leggere un retore. Riflessioni lessicali su Calpurnio Flacco", in Poignault and Schneider (2016), pp. 49–65.

Balbo, A. (2019), "Les composantes philosophiques des *Excerpta* de Calpurnius Flaccus", in S. Aubert-Baillot, C. Guérin and S. Morlet (eds), *La philosophie des non philosophes dans l'empire romain du Ier au IIIe siècle*, Paris, pp. 13–30.

Beard, M. (1993), "Looking (Harder) for Roman Myth: Dumézil, Declamation and the Problems of Definition", in F. Graf (ed.), *Mythos in mythenloser Gesellschaft. Das Paradigma Roms*, Stuttgart and Leipzig, 44–64.

Berardi, F. (2017), *La retorica degli esercizi preparatori. Glossario ragionato dei Progymnásmata*, Hildesheim, Zürich, and New York.

Bernstein, N.W. (2012), "'Torture Her until She Lies': Torture, Testimony, and Social Status in Roman Rhetorical Education", *Greece & Rome*, 59 (2): 165–177.

Bernstein, N.W. (2013a), "'Distat opus nostrum, sed fontibus exit ab isdem'. Declamation and Flavian Epic", in G. Manuwald and A. Voigt (eds), *Flavian Epic Interactions*, Berlin and Boston, pp. 139–156.

Bernstein, N.W. (2013b), *Ethics, Identity, and Community in Later Roman Declamation*, Oxford and New York.

Berti, E. (2007), *Scholasticorum Studia. Seneca il Vecchio e la cultura retorica e letteraria della prima età imperiale*, Pisa.

Berti, E. (2009), "Un frammento di una declamazione di Cicerone e due controversiae senecane", *Dictynna*, 6, http://dictynna.revue.org/247.

Berti, E. (2014), "Le *controversiae* della raccolta di Seneca il Vecchio e la dottrina degli *status*", *Rhetorica*, 32 (2): 99–147.

Berti, E. (2015), "Law in Declamation: The *status legales* in Seneca *controversiae*", in Amato, Citti, and Huelsenbeck (2015), pp. 7–62.

Bettinazzi, M. (2012), "La *lex Roscia* e la declamazione 302 ascritta a Quintiliano. Sull'uso delle declamazioni come documento dell'esperienza giuridica romana", in J-L. Ferrary (ed.), Leges publicae. *La legge nell'esperienza giuridica romana*, Pavia, pp. 515–544.

Bettinazzi, M. (2014), *La legge nelle declamazioni quintilianee. Una nuova prospettiva per lo studio della lex Voconia, della lex Iunia Norbana e della lex Iulia de adulteriis*, Saarbrücken.

Bianco, M.M. (2018), "'Prendere ad esempio'. Quando padri e figli sono innamorati (con una lettura di Sen. *contr.* II 6)", *Maia*, 70 (1): 50–72.

Bloomer, W.M. (2007), "Roman Declamation: The Elder Seneca and Quintilian", in Dominik and Hall (2007), pp. 297–306.

Borgo, A. (2014), "Tra storia e retorica: il contrasto Cicerone-Antonio nella settima suasoria di Seneca il Vecchio", in R. Grisolia and G. Matino (eds), *Arte della parola e parole della scienza. Tecniche della comunicazione letteraria nel mondo antico*, Naples, pp. 9–24.

Breij, B. (2006a), "'Post exitum unici revertor in patrem': *sententiae* in Roman Declamation", in A. Lardinois, M. van der Poel and V. Hunink (eds), *Land of Dreams: Greek and Latin Studies in Honour of A. H. M. Kessels*, Leiden and Boston, pp. 311–326.

Breij, B. (2006b), "Pseudo-Quintilian's *Major Declamations* 18 and 19: Two *controversiae figuratae*", *Rhetorica*, 24 (1): 79–105.

Breij, B. (2006c), "*Vitae necisque potestas* in Roman Declamation", *Advances in the History of Rhetoric*, 9: 55–81.

Breij, B. (2009), "Incest in Roman Declamation", in L. Pernot (ed.), *New Chapters in the History of Rhetoric*, Leiden, pp. 197–214.

Breij B. (ed.) (2015a), *[Quintilian] The Son Suspected of Incest with His Mother (Major Declamations, 18–19)*, Cassino.

Breij, B. (2015b), "The Law in the *Major Declamations* Ascribed to Quintilian", in Amato, Citti, and Huelsenbeck (2015), pp. 219–248.

Breij, B. (2016), "Rich and Poor, Father and Son in *Major Declamation 7*", in Poignault and Schneider (2016), pp. 275–290.

Breij, B. (ed.) (2020), *[Quintilian] The Poor's Man Torture (Major Declamation, 7)*, Cassino.

Breij, B. (2021), "'Inter ignes et flagella': Uses of Torture in the *Major Declamations*", in Lovato, Stramaglia, and Traina (2021), pp. 1–31.

Brescia, G. (2012), *La donna violata. Casi di* stuprum *e* raptus *nella declamazione latina*, Lecce.

Brescia, G. (2015a), "Ambiguous Silence: *stuprum* and *pudicitia* in Latin Declamation", in Amato, Citti, and Huelsenbeck (2015), pp. 75–93.

Brescia, G. (2015b), "Declamazione e mito", in M. Lentano (ed.), *La declamazione latina. Prospettive a confronto sulla retorica di scuola a Roma antica*, Naples, pp. 59–88.

Brescia, G. (2019a), "Il figlio *spes patris* nella declamazione latina e nell'immaginario letterario e giuridico", *Camenae*, 23, https://www.saprat.fr/

toutes-les-revues-en-ligne-camenae/camenae-n-23-mars-2019-declamazione-e-spettacolo-nella-tarda-antichita-192.htm.

Brescia, G. (2019b), "*Infamis in noverca. Ius occidendi* e *pietas* paterna a Roma tra retorica e diritto", *Bollettino di studi latini*, 49 (1): 44–60.

Brescia, G. (2021), "L'oracolo e il parricidio. Mito 'in filigrana' nella *Declamazione Maggiore* 4", in Lovato, Stramaglia, and Traina (2021), pp. 33–51.

Brescia, G. and Lentano, M. (2009), *Le ragioni del sangue. Storie di fratricidio e incesto nella declamazione latina*, Naples.

Brescia, G. and Lentano, M. (2016), "La norma nascosta. Storie di adulterio nella declamazione Latina", in McClintock (2016), pp. 135–184.

Brescia, G. and Lentano, M. (2020), "Suicidi infamanti e divieto di sepoltura", in A. McClintock (ed.), *Storia mitica del diritto romano*, Bologna, pp. 91–129.

Calboli, G. (2003), "Seneca il Retore tra oratoria e retorica", in I. Gualandri and G. Mazzoli (eds), *Gli Annei. Una famiglia nella storia e nella cultura di Roma imperiale. Atti del Convegno internazionale di Milano-Pavia, 2–6 maggio 2000*, Como, pp. 73–90.

Calboli, G. (2007), "Le declamazioni tra retorica, diritto, letteratura e logica", in Calboli Montefusco (2007), pp. 29–56.

Calboli, G. (2010a), "L'eros nelle declamazioni latine (una pozione di contro-amore)", *Rhetorica*, 28 (2): 138–159.

Calboli G. (2010b), "Quintilien et les déclamateurs", in P. Galand, F. Hallyn, C. Lévy, and W. Verbaal (eds), *Quintilien ancien et moderne*, Turnhout, pp. 11–28.

Calboli, G. (2016), "Les *status* et les *Petites déclamations* du Pseudo-Quintilien", in Poignault, Schneider (2016), pp. 227–239.

Calboli Montefusco, L. (1986), *La dottrina degli* status *nella retorica greca e romana*, Bologna.

Calboli Montefusco, L. (ed.) (2007), *Papers on Rhetoric, VIII. Declamation. Proceedings of the Seminars Held at the Scuola superiore di studi umanistici, Bologna (February-March 2006)*, Rome.

Canfora, L. (2015), *Augusto figlio di dio*, Rome and Bari.

Cappello, O. (2016), "*Civitas beluarum*: The Politics of Eating Your Neighbor. A Semiological Study of Ps.-Quintilian's Twelfth *Major Declamation*", in Dinter, Guérin, and Martinho (2016), pp. 209–236.

Casamento, A. (2002), "Sen. *Contr.* 2, 1, 10: una *narratio* del retore Fabiano fra suggestioni letterarie ed echi tragici", *Pan*, 20: 117–132.

Casamento, A. (2004a), "Le mani dell'eroe. In nota a Sen. *Contr.* 1,4", *Pan*, 22: 243–253.

Casamento, A. (2004b), "Nell'officina del declamatore: Metello e il salvataggio eroico del Palladio (Ov. *Fast.* 6, 437–454)", in L. Landolfi (ed.), *"Nunc teritur nostris area maior equis". Riflessioni sull'intertestualità ovidiana. I Fasti*, Palermo, pp. 103–116.

Casamento, A. (2013), "'Ignosce, non possum'. Modelli declamatori e topoi tragici a confronto: padri e figli tra declamazione e tragedia", *Pan*, n.s. 1: 95–108.
Casamento, A. (2015a), "Declamazione e letteratura", in M. Lentano (ed.), *La declamazione latina. Prospettive a confronto sulla retorica di scuola a Roma antica*, Naples, pp. 89–113.
Casamento, A. (2015b), "Il padre che dovrei essere, il padre che vorrei. Dalle declamazioni di Seneca padre alla tragedia senecana", in Poignault and Schneider (2015), pp. 215–237.
Casamento, A. (2016), "Parrasio e i limiti dell'arte. Una lettura di Sen. *Contr.* 10, 5", in L. Calboli Montefusco and M.S. Celentano (eds), *Papers on Rhetoric XIII*, Perugia, pp. 57–85.
Casamento, A. (2018), "Serve ancora uccidere i tiranni? A proposito di Ps. Quint. *decl.* 253", *Maia*, 70 (1): 84–97.
Casamento, A., van Mal-Maeder D., and Pasetti L. (eds) (2016), *Le Declamazioni minori dello Pseudo-Quintiliano. Discorsi immaginari tra letteratura e diritto*, Berlin and Boston.
Citti, F. (2007), "La declamazione greca in Seneca il Vecchio", in Calboli Montefusco (2007), pp. 57–102.
Citti, F. (2015a), "'Quaedam iura non lege, sed natura': Nature and Natural Law in Roman Declamation", in Amato, Citti, and Huelsenbeck (2015), pp. 95–131.
Citti, F. (2015b), "Serse e Demarato (*ben.* 6, 31, 1–10): Seneca, Erodoto e le declamazioni di argomento storico", *Studi italiani di filologia classica*, 4 (13): 232–249.
Citti, F. (2018), "Declamazione greca e *Romanae aures*: osservazioni sulle citazioni greche in Seneca il Vecchio", in G. Martino, F. Ficca, and R. Grisolia (eds), *Generi senza confini. La rappresentazione della realtà nel mondo antico*, Naples, pp. 57–69.
Corbeill, A. (2007), "Rhetorical Education and Social Reproduction in the Republic and Early Empire", in Dominik and Hall (2007), pp. 69–82.
Corbino, A. (2009), "'Actio in factum adversus confitentem'. Quint., *Declam. Maior* XIII", in C. Russo Ruggeri (ed.), *Studi in onore di Antonino Metro*, vol. I, Milan, pp. 511–524.
Cribiore, R. (2001), *Gymnastics of the Mind. Greek Education in Hellenistic and Roman Egypt*, Princeton, NJ and Oxford.
D'Amati, L. (2017), "*Parentes alere*: imperatori, giuristi e declamatori", *Quaderni lupiensi di storia e diritto*, 7: 143–166.
D'Amati L. (2018), "Ancora su *parentes alere*", *Roma e America. Diritto romano comune*, 39: 289–310.
Desanti, L. (2015), *La legge Aquilia. Tra verba legis e interpretazione giurisprudenziale*, Turin.
Dingel, J. (1988), Scholastica materia. *Untersuchungen zu den* Declamationes minores *und der* Institutio oratoria *Quintilians*, Berlin and New York.

Bibliography

Dinter, M.T., Guérin, C., and Martinho, M. (eds) (2016), *Reading Roman Declamation. The Declamations Ascribed to Quintilian*, Berlin and Boston.

Dinter, M.T., Guérin, C., and Martinho, M. (eds) (2017), *Reading Roman Declamation. Calpurnius Flaccus*, Berlin and Boston.

Dinter, M.T., Guérin, C., and Martinho, M. (eds) (2020), *Reading Roman Declamation. Seneca the Elder*, Oxford.

Dominik, W. and Hall, J. (eds) (2007), *A Companion to Roman Rhetoric*, Oxford.

Echavarren, A. (2007), "Los declamadores griegos en la obra de Séneca el Viejo: retrato de una minoría", in A. Sánchez-Ostiz, J. B. Torres Guerra, and R. Martínez (eds), *De Grecia a Roma y de Roma a Grecia. Un camino de ida y vuelta*, Pamplona, pp. 253–268.

Eco, U. (1994), *Sei passeggiate nei boschi narrativi*, Milan.

Enrico, M. (2021), "Contre un ennemi disparu? Tyrans et tyrannicides dans les *Déclamations* du pseudo-Quintilien", in Lovato, Stramaglia, and Traina (2021), pp. 107–121.

Fairweather, J. (1981), *Seneca the Elder*, Cambridge.

Fantham, E. (2004), "Disowning and Dysfunction in the Declamatory Family", *Materiali e discussioni per l'analisi dei testi classici*, 53: 65–82 (republ. in Fantham, *Roman Readings. Roman Response to Greek Literature from Plautus to Statius and Quintilian*, Berlin and New York (2011), pp. 302–319).

Friend, C. (1999), "Pirates, Seducers, Wronged Heirs, Poison Cups, Cruel Husbands, and Other Calamities: The Roman School Declamations and Critical Pedagogy", *Rhetoric Review*, 17 (2): 300–320.

Garbarino, G. (2003), *Philosophorum Romanorum fragmenta usque ad L. Annaei Senecae aetatem*, Bologna.

Guérin, C. (2012–13), "*Intempestiva philosophia*? Eloquence déclamatoire et éloquence philosophique au Ier siècle ap. J.-C.", *Ítaca. Quaderns Catalans de Cultura Clàssica*, 28–29: 21–43.

Guérin, C. (2018), "Des déclamateurs grecs sur la scène romaine: les enjeux de l'altérité culturelle dans les textes de Sénèque le Père", *Comptes Rendus de l'Académie des Inscriptions et Belles-Lettres*, 1: 467–489.

Guérin, C. (2020), *Greek Declaimers, Roman Context. (De)constructing Cultural Identity in Seneca the Elder*, in Dinter, Guérin, and Martinho (2020), pp. 57–86.

Gunderson, E. (2003), *Declamation, Paternity, and Roman Identity. Authority and the Rhetorical Self*, Cambridge and New York.

Håkanson, L. (ed.) (1978), *Calpurnii Flacci Declamationum excerpta*, Stuttgart.

Håkanson, L. (ed.) (1982), *Declamationes XIX maiores Quintiliano falso ascriptae*, Stuttgart.

Håkanson, L. (2014), *Unveröffentlichte Schriften*, vol. 1, *Studien zu den pseudoquintilianischen* Declamationes maiores, ed. B. Santorelli, Berlin and Boston.

Harrison, A.R.W. (2001), *Il diritto ad Atene*, 2 vols, Alessandria (first published as *The Law of Athens*, 2 vols, Oxford (1971)).

Hömke, N. (2002), *Gesetzt den Fall, ein Geist erscheint. Komposition und Motivik der ps-quintilianischen* Declamationes maiores *X, XIV und XV*, Heidelberg.

Hömke, N. (2007), "'Not to Win but to Please'. Roman Declamation beyond Education", in Calboli Montefusco (2007), pp. 103–127.

Hömke, N. (2021), "The Declaimer's Dealing with the Gruesome, Dreadful and Disgusting in *Declamationes maiores* 10 and 12", in Lovato, Stramaglia, and Traina (2021), pp. 123–140.

Huelsenbeck, B. (2018), *Figures in the Shadows. The Speech of Two Augustan-Age Declaimers, Arellius Fuscus and Papirius Fabianus*, Berlin and Boston.

Huelsenbeck, B. (2020), "The Ocean (Seneca *Suas*. 1): Community Rules for a Common Literary Topic", in Dinter, Guérin, and Martinho (2020), pp. 151–185.

Imber, M. (1997), *Tyrants and Mothers: Roman Education and Ideology*, dissertation Stanford University.

Imber, M. (2001), "Practised Speech: Oral and Written Conventions in Roman Declamation", in J. Watson (ed.), *Speaking Volumes. Orality and Literacy in the Greek and Roman World*, Leiden, Boston, MA and Köln, pp. 199–218.

Imber, M. (2008), "Life without Father: Declamation and the Construction of Paternity in the Roman Empire", in S. Bell and I.L. Hansen (eds), *Role Models in the Roman World. Identity and Assimilation*, Ann Arbor, MI, pp. 161–170.

Imber, M. (2011), *Daughters, Women and Anxious Fathers: The Function of Women in Roman Declamation*, https://bates.academia.edu/mimber.

Johansson M. (2006), *Libanius' Declamations 9 and 10*, Göteborg.

Johansson M. (2015), "Nature over Law: Themes of Disowning in Libanius' Declamations", in Amato, Citti, and Huelsenbeck (2015), pp. 269–286.

Kalospyros, N.A.E. (2016), "Towards the Formation of an Attic Genre of *declamatio*. How to Focus on Sopatros the Rhetor", in Poignault and Schneider (2016), pp. 257–274.

Kaster, R.A. (2001), "Controlling Reason. Declamation in Rhetorical Education at Rome", in Y. Lee Too (ed.), *Education in Greek and Roman Antiquity*, Leiden, pp. 317–337.

Kennedy, G.A. (2003), Progymnasmata. *Greek Textbooks of Prose Composition and Rhetoric*, Leiden and Boston.

Kohl R. (1915), *De scholasticarum declamationum argumentis ex historia petitis*, Paderborn.

Kragelund, P. (1991), "Epicurus, Pseudo-Quintilian and the Rhetor at Trajan's Forum", *Classica et Mediaevalia*, 42: 259–275.

Krapinger, G. (2016), "Die Grabverletzung in den *Declamationes minores*", in Casamento, van Mal-Maeder, and Pasetti (2016), pp. 11–30.

Krapinger, G. and Stramaglia, A. (eds) (2015), *Der Blinde auf der Türschwelle (*Größere Deklamationen, *2)*, Cassino.
Krapinger, G. and Zinsmaier, T. (2021), "Philosophische Theoreme in den *Declamationes maiores*", in Lovato, Stramaglia, and Traina (2021), pp. 141–161.
La Bua, G. (2015), "'Nihil infinitum est nisi Oceanus' (Sen. *Suas.* 1, 1). Il mare nelle declamazioni latine", *Maia*, 67 (2): 325–339.
Langer, V.I. (2007), Declamatio Romanorum. *Dokument juristischer Argumentationstechnik, Fenster in die Gesellschaft ihrer Zeit und Quelle des Rechts?*, Frankfurt am Main.
Larosa, B. (2020), "The Mythical *Exempla* of Faithful Heroines in Seneca the Elder's work: Literary Occurrences of a Declamatory Device", in Dinter, Guérin, and Martinho (2020), pp. 186–200.
Lendon, J.E. (2022), *That Tyrant, Persuasion. How Rhetoric Shaped the Roman World*, Princeton, NJ and Oxford.
Lentano, M. (1998), *L'eroe va a scuola. La figura del* vir fortis *nella declamazione latina*, Naples.
Lentano, M. (1999), "La declamazione latina. Rassegna di studi e stato delle questioni (1980–1998)", *Bollettino di studi latini*, 29 (2): 571–621.
Lentano, M. (2005), "'Un nome più grande di ogni legge'. Declamazione latina e *patria potestas*", *Bollettino di studi latini*, 35 (2): 530–561 (republ. in Lentano (2009b), pp. 45–79).
Lentano, M. (2009a), "Come uccidere un padre (della patria): Seneca e l'ingratitudine di Bruto", in G. Picone, L. Beltrami, and L. Ricottilli (eds), *Benefattori e beneficati. La relazione asimmetrica nel* de beneficiis *di Seneca*, Palermo, pp. 185–209.
Lentano, M. (2009b), Signa culturae. *Saggi di antropologia e letteratura latina*, Bologna.
Lentano, M. (2010), "La figlia del pirata. Idee per un commento a Seneca, *Controversiae* 1 6", *Annali online di Lettere – Ferrara*, 1: 89–106.
Lentano, M. (2012), "Il vascello del parricida. Un tema declamatorio tra mito e retorica (Seneca, *Controversiae*, 7, 1)", *Bollettino di studi latini*, 42 (1): 1–14.
Lentano, M. (2014a), "Musica per orecchie romane. Nota a ps.-Quint. *decl. mai.* 4, 7", *Bollettino di studi latini*, 44 (1): 166–177.
Lentano, M. (2014b), *Retorica e diritto. Per una lettura giuridica della declamazione latina*, Lecce.
Lentano, M. (ed.) (2015a), *La declamazione latina. Prospettive a confronto sulla retorica di scuola a Roma antica*, Naples.
Lentano, M. (2015b), "'Parricidii sit actio'. Killing the Father in Roman Declamation", in Amato, Citti, and Huelsenbeck (2015), pp. 133–153.
Lentano, M. (2016a), "'Auribus vestris non novum crimen'. Il tema dell'adulterio nelle *Declamationes minores*", in Casamento, van Mal-Maeder, and Pasetti (2016), pp. 63–80.

Lentano, M. (2016b), "Parlare di Cicerone sotto il governo del suo assassino. La controversia VII, 2 di Seneca e la politica augustea della memoria", in Poignault and Schneider (2016), pp. 375–391.

Lentano, M. (2017a), "Le declamazioni pseudo-quintilianee (1986–2014)", *Lustrum* 59: 131–191.

Lentano, M. (2017b), "Lo strano caso della vergine prostituta. Un dibattito sulla purezza nella cultura augustea", *Otium*, 3: 1–22.

Lentano, M. (2018a), "Cose dell'altro mondo. La figura del pirata nella cultura romana", in I.G. Mastrorosa (ed.), Latrocinium maris. *Fenomenologia e repressione della pirateria nell'esperienza romana e oltre*, Rome, pp. 173–192.

Lentano, M. (2018b), "'Onde si immolino tre vergini o più'. Un motivo mitologico nella declamazione latina", *Maia*, 70 (1): 10–27.

Lentano, M. (2019), "Confondere le tracce. L'immagine di Augusto in Seneca il Vecchio", *Invigilata lucernis*, 41: 143–160.

Lentano, M. (2021a), "Picchiatori per procura. Note esegetiche alla *Declamazione minore* 362 dello pseudo-Quintiliano", *Vichiana*, 58 (1): 69–80.

Lentano, M. (2021b), "Veder raccolto in breve spazio il mondo. Le *Declamazioni maggiori* dello pseudo-Quintiliano come collezione", in Lovato, Stramaglia, and Traina (2021), pp. 185–203.

Longo, G. (ed.) (2008), *[Quintiliano] La pozione dell'odio (Declamazioni maggiori, 14–15)*, Cassino.

Longo, G. (2016), "'Quaedam satius est causae detrimento tacere quam verecundiae dicere'. Eros 'torbido' nella declamazione latina", in Poignault and Schneider (2016), pp. 309–321.

Lovato, A., Stramaglia A. and Traina G. (eds) (2021), *Le Declamazioni maggiori pseudo-quintilianee nella Roma imperiale*, Berlin and Boston.

Lupi, S. (2010), *Coricio di Gaza, XVII (= decl. 4) F.-R.: Milziade*, Berlin and Vienna.

Mantovani, D. (2007), "I giuristi, il retore e le api. *Ius controversum* e natura nella *Declamatio Maior* XIII", in D. Mantovani and A. Schiavone (eds), *Testi e problemi del giusnaturalismo romano*, Pavia, pp. 323–385.

Mantovani, D. (2014), "Declamare le Dodici Tavole: una parafrasi di *XII Tab.* V, 3 nella *Declamatio minor* 264", *Fundamina*, 20 (2): 597–605.

Mastrorosa, I.G. (2002), "Rhetoric between Conjugal Love and *patria potestas*: Seneca the Elder, *Contr.* 2.2", in L. Calboli Montefusco (ed.), *Papers on Rhetoric IV*, Rome, pp. 165–190.

Mastrorosa, I.G. (2008), "La prosopografia della cultura retorica fra Augusto e Tiberio: in margine a uno studio recente su Seneca il Vecchio", *Bollettino di studi latini*, 38 (1): 62–74.

McClintock, A. (ed.) (2016), *Giuristi nati. Antropologia e diritto romano*, Bologna.

McClintock, A. (2022), *La ricchezza femminile e la* lex Voconia, Naples.

Migliario, E. (1989), "Luoghi retorici e realtà sociale nell'opera di Seneca il Vecchio", *Athenaeum*, 67: 525–549.

Migliario, E. (2007), *Retorica e storia. Una lettura delle* Suasorie *di Seneca Padre*, Bari.

Migliario, E. (2009), "Le proscrizioni triumvirali fra retorica e storiografia", in M.T. Zambianchi (ed.), *Ricordo di Delfino Ambaglio*, Como, pp. 55–66.

Morales, H. (2005), *Vision and Narrative in Achilles Tatius'* Leucippe and Clitophon, Cambridge.

Nicolai, R. (1996), *La storiografia nell'educazione antica*, Pisa.

Nicolai, R. (2008), "L'uso della storiografia come fonte di informazioni: teoria retorica e prassi oratoria", in J. C. Iglesias Zoido (eds), *Retórica e historiografía. El discurso militar en la historiografía desde la Antigüedad hasta el Renacimiento*, Madrid and Cáceres, pp. 143–174.

Nocchi, F.R. (2017), "Legati e mercanti nella declamazione latina", *Revue de Philologie, de Littérature et d'Histoire Anciennes*, 91 (1): 109–120.

Nocchi, F.R. (2018), "Viaggi per mare: mercanti, pirati e *mirabilia* nella declamazione latina", in R. Caldarelli and A. Boccolini (eds), *Il viaggio e l'Europa: incontri e movimenti da, verso, entro lo spazio europeo*, Viterbo, pp. 201–212.

Nocchi, F.R. (2019), "*Ambigua signa* e *signa animi*: le lacrime del tiranno", *Camenae*, 23, https://www.saprat.fr/toutes-les-revues-en-ligne-camenae/camenae-n-23-mars-2019-declamazione-e-spettacolo-nella-tarda-antichita-192.htm.

Norden, E. (1986), *La prosa d'arte antica. Dal VI secolo a.C. all'età della rinascenza*, 2 vols, Rome (original edition *Die antike Kunstprosa. Vom VI. Jahrhundert v. Chr. bis in die Zeit der Renaissance*, Leipzig (1898)).

Oppliger, C. (2016), "Quelques réflexions sur la méthode (ou les méthodes?) du Maître des *Petites déclamations*", in Casamento, van Mal-Maeder, and Pasetti (2016), pp. 103–116.

Packman, Z.M. (1999), "Rape and Consequences in the Latin Declamations", *Scholia*, 8: 17–36.

Pagán, V.E. (2007-08), "Teaching Torture in Seneca *Controversiae* 2.5", *Classical Journal*, 103 (2): 165–182.

Panayotakis, S. (2002), "The Temple and the Brothel: Mothers and Daughters in *Apollonius of Tyre*", in M. Paschalis and S. Frangoulidis (eds), *Space in the Ancient Novel*, Groningen, pp. 98–117.

Papakonstantinou, N. (2017), "'Torquete tamquam mentientem'. La déconstruction de la *quaestio* judiciaire dans la VIIe Déclamation majeure du Pseudo-Quintilien", *Camenulae*, 16: 1–14.

Paré-Rey, P. (2015), "Présence de la déclamation dans les tragédies de Sénèque", in Poignault and Schneider (2015), pp. 193–213.

Pasetti, L. (2007), "Un suicidio fallito. La topica dell'*ars moriendi* nella XVII declamazione maggiore pseudo-quintilianea", in Calboli Montefusco (2007), pp. 181–207.

Pasetti, L. (2008), "Filosofia e retorica di scuola nelle *Declamazioni Maggiori* pseudo-quintilianee", in F. Gasti and E. Romano (eds), *Retorica ed educazione delle élites nell'antica Roma. Atti della VI Giornata ghisleriana di filologia classica (Pavia, 4-5 aprile 2006)*, Pavia, pp. 113–147.

Pasetti, L. (2009), "'Mori me non vult'. Seneca and Pseudo-Quintilian's IVth *Major Declamation*", *Rhetorica*, 27 (3): 274–293.

Pasetti, L. (2015), "Cases of Poisoning in Greek and Roman Declamation", in Amato, Citti, and Huelsenbeck (2015), pp. 155–199.

Pasetti, L. (2016), "'Extra rerum naturam': retorica contro filosofia cinica nella *Declamatio minor* 283", in Casamento, van Mal-Maeder, and Pasetti (2016), pp. 81–101.

Pasetti, L. (2018), "Un tema storico nelle *Minores*. Per una lettura della *decl.* 292", *Maia*, 70: 129–139.

Pasetti, L., Casamento, A., Dimatteo, G., Krapinger, G., Santorelli, B., and Valenzano, C. (eds) (2019), *Le* Declamazioni minori *attribuite a Quintiliano*, vol. I, *244-292*, Bologna.

Penella, R.J. (2014), "Libanius' Declamations", in L. Van Hoof (ed.), *Libanius. A Critical Introduction*, Cambridge, pp. 107–127.

Pernot, L. (2007), "Il non-detto della declamazione greco-romana: discorso figurato, sottintesi e allusioni politiche", in Calboli Montefusco (2007), pp. 209–234.

Piccirilli, L. (1981), "L'*apokeryxis* di Temistocle", in *Studi in onore di Arnaldo Biscardi*, vol. I, Milan, pp. 343–355 (republ. in Piccirilli, *Temistocle, Aristide, Cimone, Tucidide di Melesia: fra politica e propaganda*, Genoa (1987), pp. 24–31).

Pingoud, J. (2020), "Dégustation de *Minores*. Le menu des suicides", in J. Pingoud and A. Rolle, *Déclamation et intertextualité. Discours d'école en dialogue*, Bern, pp. 103–206.

Pingoud, J. and Rolle A. (2016), "*Noverca* et *mater crudelis*. La perversion féminine dans les *Grandes Déclamations* à travers l'intertextualité", in Dinter, Guérin, and Martinho (2016), pp. 147–166.

Pirovano, L. (2013), "Persio e il suicidio di Catone. Sulle tracce di un esercizio scolastico antico (Pers. III 44-47)", *Erga-Logoi*, 1 (1): 41–60.

Poignault, R. and Schneider, C. (eds) (2015), *Présence de la déclamation antique (Controverses et suasoires)*, Clermont-Ferrand.

Poignault, R. and Schneider, C. (eds) (2016), *Fabrique de la déclamation antique (Controverses et suasoires)*, Lyon.

Ravallese, M. (2021), "La città che divora. Aspetti paideutici e giuridici nella XII *Declamazione maggiore* dello Pseudo-Quintiliano", in Lovato, Stramaglia, and Traina (2021), pp. 319–341.

Rizzelli, G. (2011), "'In has servandae integritatis custodias nulla libido inrumpet' (Sen. *contr.* 2.7.3). Donne, passioni, violenza", in F. Botta, F. Lucrezi, and

G. Rizzelli, *Violenza sessuale e società antiche. Profili storico-giuridici*, 2nd ed., Lecce, pp. 149–199.

Rizzelli, G. (2012), "Sen. *Contr.* 2.4 e la legislazione matrimoniale augustea. Qualche considerazione", *Index*, 40: 271–312.

Rizzelli, G. (2014a), "*Adulterium*. Immagini, etica, diritto", in F. Milazzo (ed.), *"Ubi Tu Gaius". Modelli familiari, pratiche sociali e diritti delle persone nell'età del principato. Relazioni del Convegno internazionale di diritto romano, Copanello, 4–7 giugno 2008*, Milan, pp. 145–322.

Rizzelli, G. (2014b), *Modelli di "follia" nella cultura dei giuristi romani*, Lecce.

Rizzelli, G. (2015), "Declamazione e diritto", in Lentano (2015a), pp. 211–270.

Rizzelli, G. (2016), "Tra collera e ragione. Il castigo paterno in Roma antica", in McClintock (2016), pp. 185–231.

Rizzelli, G. (2017), *Padri romani. Discorsi, modelli, norme*, Lecce.

Rizzelli, G. (2019), "Fra giurisprudenza e retorica scolastica. Note sul *ius* a Sofistopoli", *Iura & Legal Systems*, 6 (4): 102–114.

Rizzelli, G. (2021), *Il fr. 3 Stramaglia delle* Declamazioni maggiori *e la circolazione di temi fra retori e giuristi*, in Lovato, Stramaglia, and Traina (2021), pp. 343–360.

Rolle, A. (2018), "L'importanza del confronto. Un'analisi di Sen. *contr.* x 4, 23", *Maia*, 70 (1): 42–49.

Romeo, A. (2018), "Il mito di Cefalo e Procri e il mito della prova di fedeltà (Ov. *Met.* 7,720-746)", *Paideia*, 73 (3): 2013–2031.

Russell, D.A. (1983), *Greek Declamation*, Cambridge.

Santorelli, B. (ed.) (2014), *[Quintiliano] Il ricco accusato di tradimento (*Declamazioni maggiori, *11). Gli amici garanti (*Declamazioni maggiori, *16)*, Cassino.

Santorelli, B. (2016a), "Il denaro negato. Casi di *infitiatio depositi* nelle *Declamazioni minori*", in Casamento, van Mal-Maeder, and Pasetti (2016), pp. 31–46.

Santorelli, B. (2016b), "Juvenal and Declamatory *inventio*", in A. Stramaglia, S. Grazzini, and G. Dimatteo (eds), *Giovenale tra storia, poesia e ideologia*, Berlin and Boston, pp. 293–321.

Santorelli, B. (2017), "Metrical and Accentual *clausulae* as Evidence for the Date and Origin of Calpurnius Flaccus", in Dinter, Guérin, and Martinho (2017), pp. 129–140.

Santorelli, B. (2019), "'Poteram quidem fortiter dicere: "Pater iussi"'. L'autorità paterna a scuola tra retorica e diritto", in L. Capogrossi Colognesi, F. Cenerini, F. Lamberti, M. Lentano, G. Rizzelli, and B. Santorelli (eds), *Anatomie della paternità. Padri e famiglia nella cultura romana*, Lecce, pp. 73–88.

Santorelli, B. (2021), "Datazione e paternità delle *Declamazioni maggiori* pseudo-quintilianee", in Lovato, Stramaglia, and Traina (2021), pp. 361–429.

Santorelli, B. and Stramaglia, A. (2015), "La declamazione perduta", in Lentano (2015a), pp. 271–304.

Schneider, C. (2000), "Quelques réflexions sur la date de publication des *Grandes déclamations* pseudo-quintiliennes", *Latomus*, 59 (3): 614–632.

Schouler, B. (1984), *La tradition hellénique chez Libanios*, 2 vols, Paris.

Schwartz, P. (2016), "Tyrans et tyrannicides dans les *Petites déclamations*", in Dinter, Guérin, and Martinho (2016), pp. 267–278.

Sciortino, S. (2003), "C. 8.46.6: Brevi osservazioni in tema di *abdicatio* ed *APOKHRYXIS*", *Annali del Seminario giuridico dell'Università di Palermo*, 48: 335–378.

Shackleton Bailey, R.D. (ed.) (2006), *Quintilian. The Lesser Declamations*, 2 vols, Cambridge, MA and London.

Stagl, J.F. (2012), "La 'Lis de dotibus socrus et nurus' e il potere del *favor dotis* (Quint. decl. 360), *Index*, 40: 326–341 (also "Durch Rede zum Recht am Beispiel von Quint. Decl. 360", *Journal on European History of Law*, 4 (2013): 2–9).

Stramaglia, A. (ed.) (1999), *[Quintiliano] I gemelli malati: un caso di vivisezione* (Declamazioni maggiori, *8*), Cassino.

Stramaglia, A. (ed.) (2003), *[Quintiliano] La città che si cibò dei suoi cadaveri* (Declamazioni maggiori, *12*), Cassino.

Stramaglia, A. (2006), "Le *Declamationes maiores* pseudo-quintilianee: genesi di una raccolta declamatoria e fisionomia della sua trasmissione testuale", in E. Amato (ed.), *Approches de la Troisième Sophistique. Hommages à Jacques Schamp*, Brussels, pp. 555–584.

Stramaglia, A. (2010), "Come si insegnava a declamare? Riflessioni sulle "routines" scolastiche dell'insegnamento retorico antico", in L. Del Corso and O. Pecere (eds), *Libri di scuola e pratiche didattiche dall'Antichità al Rinascimento. Atti del Convegno internazionale di studi, Cassino, 7-10 maggio 2008*, Cassino, pp. 111–151.

Stramaglia, A. (ed.) (2013), *[Quintiliano] L'astrologo* (Declamazioni maggiori, *4*), Cassino.

Stramaglia, A. (2015), "Temi 'sommersi' e trasmissione dei testi nella declamazione antica (con un regesto di papiri declamatori)", in L. Del Corso, F. De Vivo, and A. Stramaglia (eds), *Nel segno del testo. Edizioni, materiali e studi per Oronzo Pecere*, Florence, pp. 147–178.

Stramaglia, A. (2016a), "Il maestro nascosto. Elementi "metaretorici" nelle *Declamazioni maggiori* pseudo-quintilianee", in Poignault and Schneider (2016), pp. 21–47 (*The Hidden Teacher. "Metarhetoric" in Ps.-Quintilian's Major Declamations*, in Dinter, Guérin, and Martinho (2016), pp. 25–48).

Stramaglia, A. (2016b), "Out of Fashion? A Neglected Declamatory Theme in the Elder Seneca", in J.C. Montes Cala, L.J. Gallé Cejudo, M. Sánchez Ortiz de Landaluce, and T. Silva Sánchez (eds), *Fronteras entre el verso y la prosa en la literatura helenística y helenístico-romana. Homenaje al Prof. José Guillermo Montes Cala*, Bari, pp. 671–678.

Bibliography

Stramaglia, A. (2017), "I frammenti delle *Declamazioni maggiori* pseudo-quintilianee", *Studi italiani di filologia classica*, s. IV, 15: 195–214.

Stramaglia, A. (ed.) (2021), *Quintilian. The Major Declamations*, 3 vols, Cambridge, MA and London.

Sussman, L.A. (1995), "Sons and Fathers in the *Major Declamations* Ascribed to Quintilian", *Rhetorica*, 13 (2): 179–192.

Tabacco, R. (1985), *Il tiranno nelle declamazioni di scuola in lingua latina*, Turin.

Thomas, Y. (1983), "Paura dei padri e violenza dei figli: immagini retoriche e norme di diritto", in E. Pellizer and N. Zorzetti (eds), *La paura dei padri nella società antica e medievale*, Rome and Bari, pp. 113–140.

Torri, M. (2002-2003), "La réception de la propagande d'Auguste chez Sénèque le Rhéteur", *Classica*, 15–16: 117–130.

Traina, G. (2021), "Le *Declamazioni maggiori*: istruzioni agli storici", in Lovato, Stramaglia, and Traina (2021), pp. 431–448.

Valenzano, C. (2016), "Matrigne, avvelenatrici, donne incestuose: il paradigma di Medea nelle *Declamationes minores*", in Casamento, van Mal-Maeder, and Pasetti (2016), pp. 117–136.

Valenzano, C. (2019), "L'adulterio nella declamazione latina: un'indagine di alcuni paradigmi tragici", *Studi classici e orientali*, 65: 269–282.

van der Poel, M. (2009), "The Use of *exempla* in Roman Declamation", *Rhetorica*, 27 (3): 332–353.

van Mal-Maeder, D. (2003), "'Credibiles fabulas fecimus': mythe, rhétorique et fiction dans les déclamations latines", in M. Guglielmo and E. Bona (eds), *Forme di comunicazione nel mondo antico e metamorfosi del mito: dal teatro al romanzo*, Alessandria, pp. 187–200.

van Mal-Maeder, D. (2004), "Sénèque le tragique et les *Grandes déclamations* du Pseudo-Quintilien. Poétique d'une métamorphose", in M. Zimmerman and R. van der Paardt (eds), *Metamorphic Reflections. Essays Presented to Ben Hijmans at His 75th Birthday*, Leuven and Dudley, MA, pp. 189–199.

van Mal-Maeder, D. (2007), *La fiction des déclamations*, Leiden and Boston.

van Mal-Maeder D. (2012), "Les beaux principes. Du discours à l'action dans le *Satyricon* de Pétrone", *Ancient Narrative*, 10: 1–10.

van Mal-Maeder, D. (2018a), "Quand Démosthène déclame en latin. Ps. Quint. *decl.* 339", *Maia*, 70 (1): 140–148.

van Mal-Maeder, D. (ed.) (2018b), *[Quintilien] Le malade racheté (Grandes déclamations, 5)*, Cassino.

Vesley, M.E. (2003), "Father–Son Relations in Roman Declamation", *The Ancient History Bulletin*, 17: 159–180.

Visonà, L. (2021), "Personaggi storici nella declamazione latina: qualche riflessione su Alessandro Magno", in Lovato, Stramaglia, and Traina (2021), pp. 461–472.

Vössing, K. (2010), "Der Kaiser und die Deklamationen", in Y. Perrin (ed.), *Neronia VIII. Bibliothèques, livres et culture écrite dans l'empire romain de César à Hadrien. Actes du VIIIe Colloque international de la SIEN (Paris, 2–4 octobre 2008)*, Brussels, pp. 301–314.

Webb, R. (2006), "Fiction, *mimesis* and the Performance of the Greek Past in the Second Sophistic", in D. Konstan and S. Saïd (eds), *Greeks on Greekness. Viewing the Greek Past under the Roman Empire*, Cambridge, pp. 27–46.

Winterbottom, M. (1983), "Declamation, Greek and Latin", in Ars rhetorica *antica e nuova*, Genoa, pp. 56–76 (republ. in Winterbottom (2019), pp. 103–118).

Winterbottom, M. (ed.) (1984), *The Minor Declamations Ascribed to Quintilian*, Berlin and New York.

Winterbottom, M. (1988), "Introduction", in D. Innes and M. Winterbottom, *Sopatros the Rhetor. Studies in the Text of the Διαίρεσις Ζητημάτων*, London, pp. 1–20 (republ. in Winterbottom (2019), pp. 135–160).

Winterbottom, M. (2006), "Declamation and Philosophy", *Classica (Brasil)*, 19: 74–82 (republ. in Winterbottom (2019), pp. 243–251).

Winterbottom, M. (2018), "The Words of the Master", *Maia*, 70: 73–83 (republ. in Winterbottom (2019), pp. 283–294).

Winterbottom, M. (2019), *Papers on Quintilian and Ancient Declamation*, ed. A. Stramaglia, F.R. Nocchi, and G. Russo, Oxford and New York.

Wycisk, T. (2008), *"Quidquid in foro fieri potest". Studien zum römischen Recht bei Quintilian*, Berlin.

Zinsmaier, T. (ed.) (2009), *Die Hände der blinden Mutter (Größere Deklamationen, 6)*, Cassino.

Zinsmaier, T. (2015), *Truth by Force? Torture as Evidence in Ancient Rhetoric and Roman Law*, in Amato, Citti, and Huelsenbeck (2015), pp. 201–218.

INDEX

Abdicatio (disownment) 25–28, 32, 34, 44, 56, 63, 67, 72, 81–82, 85
Adultery 12–13, 29, 32, 36–37, 74, 76–77, 79, 88
Apokéryxis (disownment) 26, 34, 82, 85

Civil war 32, 45, 48, 59, 64
Color (colour) 11
Comedy 52, 54, 58
Constitutio, see *Status*

Declamatory laws:
   Actio ingrati 65, 69, 73, 74, n. 3
   Actio inscripti maleficii 49
   Adulterum cum adultera qui deprehenderit, dum utrumque corpus interficiat, sine fraude sit 12 & n. 18, 32, 77–78, 88
   Damni per iniuriam dati sit actio 75, 76 & n. 7
   De moribus sit actio 46 & n. 26, 65
   Incesta saxo deiciatur 12 & n. 17
   Indemnatos liberos liceat occidere 69 & n. 27, 70, 72, 87
   Liberi parentes alant aut vinciantur 11, 13, 73 & n. 2
   Liberi parentes in calamitate ne deserant 21, 70, 73 & n. 2
   Liceat adulterium in matre et filio vindicare 12 & n. 17
   Malae tractationis sit actio 69 & nn. 25–26, 87
   Mariti bona uxor accipiat 20 & n. 8, 21
   Parricidae insepulti abiciantur 55 & n. 52
   Parricidii sit actio 29
   Qui patrem pulsaverit, manus ei praecidantur 73 & n. 2
   Qui ter fortiter fecerit, militia vacet 13 & n. 22, 81–84, 86
   Rapta raptoris mortem aut indotatas nuptias optet 12 & n. 19, 70, 72
   Raptor, nisi et suum pater exoraverit et raptae intra triginta dies, pereat 68 & n. 21
   Sacerdos casta e castis, pura e puris sit 11, 12 & n. 16, 53–54
   Sepulcri violati sit actio 55 & n. 52
   Tyrannicidae praemium 39, 62–63
   Viro forti praemium 25, 30, 39, 62–63, 68
Dementia (madness) 25, 40, 42, 48, 67–69, 73
Divisio (division) 11, 23, 81

Epic 14, 53 n. 45, 65
Exemplum (example) 17, 45, 47, 51, 86

Father–son relationship 13–14, 21–22, 24–34, 38–42, 48–49, 55–56, 62–63, 67–70, 72–73, 80–87

Greek declamation 3, 6, 14, 34–35, 38, 46, 84
Greek law 34, 73, 77, 82, 85
Greek rhetoricians and declaimers 3, 6–9, 26, 46, 81–90

Historiography 8, 44, 45, 47, 48, 66
Husband–wife relationship 21, 24, 31–33, 36–37, 62–63, 67, 69–70, 74, 77–79, 87–88

Incest 14, 24, 29 & n. 16, 31, 69

Mother–son relationship 13, 21, 29, 31–32, 39, 42, 47, 53, 69–70, 74, 86–87
Myth 10, 44, 46, 53–57, 61–62

Novel 14, 52, 53 & n. 45, 54, 57

Patria potestas (paternal power) 67, 70, 85
Patricide 14, 19, 29, 33, 39, 41, 46, 47, 51, 55, 56, 57, 74
Philosophy 6, 41–44, 58, 89
Pirates 11–15, 21, 25, 29, 35, 37–39, 52–58, 80, 83–84, 87
Poison, poisoning 14, 19, 20, 53, 55, 76, 89
Progymnasmata (*praeexercitamina*) (preliminary exercises) 8

Rape 12, 20, 21, 35, 38, 67, 68, 72
Relationship between brothers 24, 26, 30, 33, 35, 56, 83
Rich and poor 25, 34–35, 75–76, 89
Roman laws:
   Lex Aquilia de damno 76
   Lex Iulia de adulteriis coercendis 77–78
   Lex Iulia de maritandis ordinibus 63
   Lex Voconia 35, 50

Sermo (discussion) 20, 21, 40
Slave 35, 38, 42–43, 66–68, 71

Status 11, 17–23
   Ambiguitas 18
   Comparatio 18
   Concessio 18
   Ratiocinatio (*syllogismus*) 18
   Relatio (*translatio*) *criminis* 18
   Remotio criminis 18
   Status coniecturalis (*coniectura*) 18, 22
   Status finitivus (*finitio*) 18, 21, 54, 79, 88
   Status incidentes 23
   Status legales 17, 79
   Status legum contrariarum 18, 79
   Status qualitatis (*qualitas*) 18
   Status rationales 17, 18, 20, 22
   Status scripti et sententiae (*scripti et voluntatis*) 18, 19, 22, 79, 88
   Translatio (*praescriptio*) 18
Stepmother 14–15, 24, 30–31, 39, 79–80, 89
Stepson 14, 24, 31
Suicide 21, 32, 41, 74

Tirocinium fori (legal apprenticeship) 7
Torture 31, 38 & n. 39, 57, 69
Tragedy 14–15, 52, 53 & n. 45, 54 & n. 51, 56, 61–63, 79
Tyrant (tyrannicide) 13–15, 31, 38 & n. 38, 39, 46, 61–63, 67–68, 79–80, 83–84, 87

Vir fortis (war hero) 12, n. 18, 13–14, 25, 30, 39, 41, 63, 80–82, 84
Vitae necisque potestas (*ius vitae necisque*) (power over life and death) 27–28, 72, 84

Printed in the USA
CPSIA information can be obtained
at www.ICGtesting.com
JSHW021859081023
49707JS00001B/2